THE OCCULT WORLD

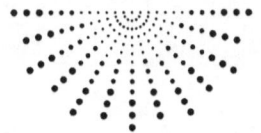

ALFRED PERCY SINNETT

To one whose comprehension of Nature and Humanity ranges so far beyond the science and philosophy of Europe, that only the broadest-minded representatives of either will be able to realise the existence of such powers in Man as those he constantly exercises,—to

THE MAHATMA KOOT HOOMI,

whose gracious friendship has given the present writer his title to claim the attention of the European world, this little volume, with permission sought and obtained, is affectionately dedicated.

A.P. Sinnett.

CONTENTS

PREFACE TO THE AMERICAN EDITION	1
INTRODUCTION	6
OCCULTISM AND THE ADEPTS	15
THE THEOSOPHICAL SOCIETY	23
FIRST OCCULT EXPERIENCES	32
TEACHINGS OF OCCULT PHILOSOPHY	99
LATER OCCULT PHENOMENA	111
APPENDIX	132

PREFACE TO THE AMERICAN EDITION

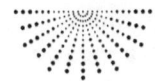

I VENTURE to think that this volume has acquired an importance that did not attach to it at first, now that subsequent experience has enabled me to follow it up with a more elaborate philosophical treatise. In the later work I have endeavored to set forth the general outlines of that knowledge concerning the higher mysteries of Nature which the following pages describe as possessed by the Indian "Mahatmas," or Adept Brothers. To that later work the reader whose attention may be arrested by the story told here must of course be referred; but meanwhile, the present introduction to the subject may be recommended to public notice now in a more confident tone than that which I was justified in taking up when it was first put forward. At that time the experiences I felt impelled to relate embodied no absolute promise of the systematic teaching accorded to me afterwards. Certainly those experiences in themselves appeared to me to claim telling. They seemed by far too remarkable to be left buried unfruitfully in the consciousness of the few persons concerned with them. It was true they elucidated no great principles of science; they merely suggested that for some of the abnormal phenomena which have arrested public attention during the last few years a more scientific explanation than those usually assigned might be possible. They afforded, if not absolute proof, at least an overwhelming assumption, that living men might actually develop faculties qualified to operate freely on that superior plane of Nature beyond the reach of the physical senses which, had been generally supposed accessible only to the spirits of the dead. But all was still shadowy and ill-defined. The story I had to tell revealed a magnificent possibility rather than a definite prospect. It would still, perhaps, have been an interesting story, even if the curtain had gone down upon the situation as I left it when these pages were first put together, but it would have been nothing then, compared to what it has since become.

Now the position in which the subject stands has altogether changed. The tentative communications addressed to me by my Mahatma correspondent in the first instance have paved the way for a long series of still more instructive and valuable letters. Assisted in other ways as well, my comprehension of occult philosophy advanced so far during the two years following the first appearance of this volume, that I was enabled to publish a more important statement, defining the outlines of that teaching, and exhibiting in a connected and intelligible shape the great esoteric theory of human evolution on this earth (and of the cosmogony on which it depends) with which the Adepts deal. The opening which presented itself to me in 1880 proved, in fact, no passing adventure, but the beginning of a new intellectual life. Attracted to it as I was at the time, I was certainly far then from divining the magnitude of the results destined to flow from it. But now that the proportions of the revelation I have thus been happily instrumental in procuring for the service of my readers have become apparent, I revert to the introductory episode of the undertaking with the certain assurance that I shall be engaging no one who will spare me his attention in any waste of time.

I am bold enough to say this because the Mahatmas, or great philosophical teachers of Asia, into some relations with whom I was enabled to come under the circumstances described in the following narrative, have now surrendered to the outer world so much of the spiritual science they have hitherto jealously guarded, that the whole framework of their stupendous doctrine has grown intelligible. Fragments of esoteric truth—of that science of superphysical nature which the Adepts explore—have been thrown out into the world at large from time to time before now, but in puzzling and unattractive disguises. The esoteric doctrine is no new system of belief, but, on the contrary, can be discerned now as lurking in a good deal of old Kabalistic and Oriental literature, that very few ordinary readers could have made sense of without the help of the keys now put in their hands. But now at last the subject has emerged into the clear daylight of modern thinking, and the central principle of the sublime esoteric doctrine stands plainly revealed as one which harmonizes in absolute perfection with the preparatory conceptions of Nature that have been derived by physical science from the observation and reflection of the current century. Biology is the latest, and, in some respects, the greatest of the physical sciences; and as the corollary, the complement, the crown of the science of Life, we are now furnished, by the teaching that has come to us from the East, with the science of spiritual evolution. Without this it may now be seen by those who appreciate the necessity of this doctrine, —the manifest, inherent self-evidence of it when it is once fairly understood, —without it, the doctrine of physical evolution is a libel on Nature, a caricature of her grandest purposes. The great idea to which I am now referring exhibits the human soul as a continuous entity, subject to an individual evolution of vast duration, and developing on the spiritual plane of existence, as a result of its successive returns to Earth life. Mounting always upward, it has passed through the lower manifestations of the animal kingdom, and can never again revert to them; but as regards the future, it will not merely pass through a purposeless succession of human lives like those going on around us. It will advance and expand in its individual progress towards perfection, *pari passu* with that general improvement of physical types on Earth which is still going forward, though the short views of human nature afforded us by mere historic observation may not render this process of improvement as perceptible to uninitiated intelligence as it becomes to the psychic discernment of the Adept.

To comprehend the way the work goes on, we have to contemplate the operations of Nature on other planes besides those cognizable to the physical senses. And it soon becomes apparent that the physical life of the Earth is only one process of the long series over which the evolution of humanity extends. But—and this is one of the most admirably scientific and ethically beautiful of the ideas brought out by occult study—the physical life of the Earth is shown to be no incoherent episode in the experiences of a human soul, no futile incident in the course of a spiritual evolution, the major portion of which is accomplished in higher spheres of being. It is inseparably blended along its whole course with the spiritual growth of the soul. The Earth is shown to be no cosmic railway carriage which we enter for the purpose of accomplishing a more or less laborious journey, and the discomforts of which we may carelessly forget when we are able to jump out of it on reaching our destination. It is the home of our race for a long time to come, if not for eternity, and it is our interest, as well as our duty, to embellish and improve and ennoble it. "In my Father's house," says the old symbolical text, "are many mansions," and in this planetary house of humanity there are many more states of existence than the physical state. Some of these states may be far more enjoyable, for that matter, than the physical state as this is at present; and the esoteric doctrine shows us that the duration of the higher spiritual states, when each individual Ego passes each time into these, is enormously more prolonged than its physical states, but both kinds of existence are equally necessary in the whole scheme of things.

All these views, and the vast mass of explanatory detail which has since been furnished to the inquirers of the Theosophical Society, were still undeveloped for those of us who were pursuing the clue afforded by my experiences of 1880, when the present book was written. But I refer to them here because I want very briefly to indicate the direction which our later inquiries took when, our attention having been arrested by the strange and startling phenomena here described, it dawned upon us by degrees that the intellectual instruction the Mahatmas could give us, if they would, would be enormously more interesting than even the exhibition of their abnormal powers. The same considerations I hope will follow in due order, in the case of readers whom this volume may have the good fortune to attract. It has been sometimes argued in my hearing that it would have been better if the authors of this great new movement of spiritual thought—new for us, though so old in one sense—which theosophy embodies had furnished us with the results of their philosophical thinking without impairing the pure dignity of that exalted scheme by mingling it in the first instance with sensational displays of thaumaturgic skill. I am not inclined myself to quarrel with the order in which events were actually unfolded, Miracles, it is quite true, are illogical guarantees for theological dogma; but the manifest possession of great faculties and powers in other planes of Nature than those on which ordinary conclusions concerning her processes are formed, does certainly afford a presumption that persons so endowed may gather observations on those higher planes which it is well worth our while to correlate with our own. Meanwhile, I do not put forward the narrative of occult phenomena, of which this volume largely consists, as a statement which in itself constitutes a foundation for the very stupendous edifice of doctrines which later opportunities enabled me to construct. But I know that the experiences I record in this book were neither futile nor fruitless in their effects on my own development; and in anticipation of events that may contribute in no small degree, in a near future, to give a great impetus to theosophic speculation in America, I venture to recommend this book with special urgency to the American public, in the hope that a reflection on their minds of the influence produced on my own, by the incidents described, may serve to attract a good many fresh explorers into the paths of study and meditation, in which I believe myself to have gained such inestimable advantage.

I have not found much to alter in the original text of this book, though I am glad to, take advantage of this opportunity to append some notes here and there, and amplify some passages. But important additions to its contents have been made from time to time, and now especially I am anxious to call the attention of American readers to the latest of these, which will be found in an appendix. It is possible that in America some persons, to whom the existence of theosophy as a new school of thought is not altogether strange, may have heard of it especially in connection with a correspondence which has attracted a good deal of attention in the spiritualistic press. The discussion to which I refer has borne reference to a manifest identity of language traced between a certain passage in one of my Mahatma teacher's letters and a similar passage in an address delivered a few years ago by an American lecturer. The explanation I am now enabled to give of the curious circumstances under which this state of things arose, constitutes in itself, I venture to think, not merely a complete refutation of some unfriendly theories which were started to account for it, but also affords a very interesting contribution to our acquaintanceship with the ways and faculties of the Mahatmas.

INTRODUCTION

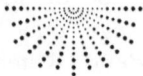

THERE is a school of Philosophy still in existence of which modern culture has lost sight. Glimpses of it are discernible in the ancient philosophies with which all educated men are familiar, but these are hardly more intelligible than fragments of forgotten sculpture,—less so, for we comprehend the human form, and can give imaginary limbs to a torso; but we can give no imaginary meaning to the truth coming down to us from Plato or Pythagoras, pointing, for those who hold the clue to their significance, to the secret knowledge of the ancient world. Side lights, nevertheless, may enable us to decipher such language, and a very rich intellectual reward offers itself to persons who are willing to attempt the investigation.

For, strange as the statement will appear at first sight, modern metaphysics, and to a large extent modern physical science, have been groping for centuries blindly after knowledge which occult philosophy has enjoyed in full measure all the while. Owing to a train of fortunate circumstances, I have come to *know* that this is the case; I have come into some contact with persons who are heirs of a greater knowledge concerning the mysteries of Nature and humanity than modern culture has yet evolved; and my present wish is to sketch the outlines of this knowledge, to record with exactitude the experimental proofs I have obtained that occult science invest its adepts with a control of natural forces superior to that enjoyed by physicists of the ordinary type, and the grounds there are for bestowing the most respectful consideration on the theories entertained by occult science concerning the constitution and destinies of the human soul. Of course people in the present day will be slow to believe that any knowledge worth considering can be found outside the bright focus of Western culture. Modern science has accomplished grand results by the open method of investigation, and is very impatient of the theory that persons who ever attained to real knowledge, either in sciences or metaphysics, could have been content to hide their light under a bushel. So the tendency has been to conceive that occult philosophers of old-Egyptian priests, Chaldean Magi, Essenes, Gnostics, theurgic Neo-Platonists, and the rest—who kept their knowledge secret, must have adopted that policy to conceal the fact that they knew very little. Mystery can only have been loved by charlatans who wished to mystify. The conclusion is pardonable from the modern point of view, but it has given rise to an impression in the popular mind that the ancient mystics have actually been turned inside out, and found to know very little. This impression is absolutely erroneous. Men of science in former ages worked in secret, and instead of publishing their discoveries, taught them in secret to carefully selected pupils. Their motives for adopting that policy are readily intelligible, even if the merits of the policy may seem still open to discussion. At all events, their teaching has not been forgotten; it has been transmitted by secret initiation to men of our own time, and while its methods and its practical achievements remain secrets in their hands, it is open to any patient and earnest student of the question to satisfy himself that these methods are of supreme efficacy, and these achievements far more admirable than any yet standing to the credit of modern science.

For the secrecy in which these operations have been shrouded has never disguised their existence, and it is only in our own time that this has been forgotten. Formerly at great public ceremonies, the initiates displayed the powers with which their knowledge of natural laws invested them. We carelessly assume that the narratives of such displays describe performances of magic: we have decided that there is no such thing as magic, therefore the narratives must have been false, the persons whom they refer to, impostors. But supposing that magic, of old, was simply the science of magi, of learned men, there is no magic, in the modern sense, left in the matter. And supposing that such science —even in ancient times already the product of long ages of study— had gone in some directions further than our much younger modern science has yet reached, it is reasonable to conclude that some displays in connection with ancient mysteries may have been strictly scientific experiments, though they sound like displays of magic, and would look like displays of magic for us now if they could be repeated.

On that hypothesis modern sagacity applying modern knowledge to the subject of ancient mysteries, may be merely modern folly evolving erroneous conclusions from modern ignorance.

But there is no need to construct hypotheses in the matter. The facts are accessible if they are sought for in the right way, and the facts are these: The wisdom of the ancient world—science and religion commingled, physics and metaphysics combined—was a reality, and it still survives. It is that which will be spoken of in these pages as Occult Philosophy. It was already a complete system of knowledge that had been cultivated in secret, and handed down to initiates for ages, before its professors performed experiments in public to impress the popular mind in Egypt and Greece. Adepts of occultism in the present day are capable of performing similar experiments, and of exhibiting results that prove them immeasurably further advanced than ordinary modern science in a comprehension of the forces of Nature. Furthermore, they inherit from their great predecessors a science which deals not merely with physics, but with the constitution and capacities of the human soul and spirit. Modern science has discovered the circulation of the blood; occult science understands the circulation of the life-principle. Modern physiology deals with the body only; occultism with the soul as well—not as the subject of vague, religious rhapsodies; but it is an actual entity, with properties that can be examined in combination with, or apart from, those of the body.

It is chiefly in the East that occultism is still kept up in India and in adjacent countries. It is in India that I have encountered it; and this little volume is written to describe the experiences I have enjoyed, and to retail the knowledge I have acquired.

II

My narrative of events must be preceded by some further general explanations, or it would be unintelligible. The identity of occultism as practised in all ages, must be kept in view, to account for the magnitude of its organization, and for the astounding discovery that secluded Orientals may understand more about electricity than Faraday, more about physics than Tyndall. The culture of Europe has been developed by Europeans for themselves within the last few hundred years. The culture of occultists is the growth of vast periods long anterior to these, when civilization inhabited the East. And during a career which has carried occultism in the domain of physical science far beyond the point we have reached, physical science has merely been an object for occultism of secondary importance. Its main strength has been devoted to metaphysical inquiry, and to the latent psychological faculties in man, faculties which, in their development, enable the occultist to obtain actual experimental knowledge concerning the soul's condition of extra-corporeal existence. There is thus something more than a mere archaeological interest in the identification of the occult system with the doctrines of the initiated organisations in all ages of the world's history, and we are presented by this identification with the key to the philosophy of religious development. Occultism is not merely an isolated discovery showing humanity to be possessed of certain powers over Nature, which the narrower study of Nature from the merely materialistic standpoint has failed to develop; it is an illumination cast over all previous spiritual speculation worth anything, of a kind which knits together some apparently divergent systems. It is to spiritual philosophy much what Sanskrit was found to be to comparative philology; it is a common stock of philosophical roots. Judaism, Christianity, Buddhism and the Egyptian theology are thus brought into one family of ideas. Occultism, as it is no now invention, is no specific sect, but the professors of no sect can afford to dispense with the sidelights it throws upon the conception of Nature and Man's destinies which they may have been induced by their own specific faith to form; occultism, in fact, must be recognised by anyone who will take the trouble to put before his mind clearly the problems with which it deals, as a study of the most sublime importance to every man who cares to live a life worthy of his human rank in creation, and who can realise the bearing on ethics of certain knowledge concerning his own survival after death. It is one thing to follow the lead of a hazy impression that a life beyond the grave, if there is one, may be somehow benefited by abstinence from wrongdoing on this side; it will clearly be another to realise if that can be shown to be the case, that the life beyond the grave must, with the certainty of a sum total built up of a series of plus and minus quantities, be the final expression of the use made of opportunities in this.

I have said that the startling importance of occult knowledge turns on the manner in which it affords exact and experimental knowledge concerning spiritual things which under all other systems must remain the subject of speculation or blind religious faith. It may be further asserted that occultism shows that the harmony and smooth continuity of Nature observable in physics extend to those operations of Nature that are concerned with the phenomena of metaphysical existence.

Before approaching an exposition of the conclusions concerning the nature of man that occult philosophy has reached, it may be worth while to meet an objection that may perhaps be raised by the reader on the threshold of the subject. How is it that conclusions of such great weight have been kept the secret property of a jealous body of initiates? Is it not a law of progress that truth asserts itself and courts the free air and light? Is it reasonable to suppose that the greatest of all truths—the fundamental basis of truth concerning man and Nature—should be afraid to show itself? With what object could the ancient professors of, or proficients in, occult philosophy keep the priceless treasures of their researches to themselves?

Now, it is no business of mine to defend the extreme tenacity with which the proficients in occultism have hitherto not only shut out the world from the knowledge of their knowledge, but have almost left it in ignorance that such knowledge exists. It is enough here to point out that it would be foolish to shut our eyes to a revelation that may now be partially conceded, merely because we are piqued at the behaviour of those who have been in a position to make it before, but have not chosen to do so. Nor would it be wiser to say that the reticence of the occultists so far discredits anything we may now be told about their acquirements. When the sun is actually shining it is no use to say that its light is discredited by the behaviour of the barometer yesterday. I have to deal, in discussing the acquirements of occultism, with facts that have actually taken place, and nothing can discredit what is known to be true. No doubt it will be worth while later on to examine the motives which have rendered the occultists of all ages so profoundly reserved. And there may be more to say in justification of the course that has been pursued than is visible at the first glance. Indeed, the reader will not go far in an examination of the nature of the powers which proficients in occultism actually possess, without seeing that it is supremely desirable to keep back the practical exercise of such powers from the world at large. But it is one thing to deny mankind generally the key which unlocks the mystery of occult power; it is another to withhold the fact that there is a mystery to unlock. However, the further discussion of that question here would be premature. Enough for the present to take note of the fact that secrecy after all is not complete if external students of the subject are enabled to learn as much about the mysteries as I shall have to tell. Manifestly, there is a great deal more behind, but, at all events, a great deal is to be learned by inquirers who will set to work in the right way.

And that which may now be learned is no new revelation at last capriciously extended to the outer world for the first time. In former periods of history, a great deal more has been known about the nature of occultism by the world at large than is known at this moment to the modern West. The bigotry of modem civilization, and not the jealousy of the occultist, is to blame if the European races are at this moment more generally ignorant of the extent to which psychological research has been carried, than the Egyptian populace in the past, or the people of India in the present day. As regards the latter, amongst whom the truth of the theory just suggested can easily be put to the test, you will find the great majority of Hindus perfectly convinced of the truth of the main statements which I am about to put forward. They do not generally or readily talk about such subjects with Europeans, because these are so prone to stupid derision of views they do not understand or believe in already. The Indian native is very timid in presence of such ridicule. But it does not affect in the slightest degree the beliefs which rest in his own mind on the fundamental teaching he will always have received, and in many cases on odds and ends of experiences he may himself have had. The Hindus are thus well aware, as a body, of the fact that there are persons who by entire devotion to certain modes of life acquire unusual powers in the nature of such as Europeans would very erroneously call supernatural. They are quite familiar with the notion that such persons live secluded lives, and are inaccessible to ordinary curiosity, and that they are nonetheless approachable by fit and determined candidates for admission to occult training. Ask any cultivated Hindu if he has ever heard of Mahatmas and Yog Vidya or occult science, and it is a hundred to one that you will find he has—and, unless he happens to be one of the hybrid products of Anglo-Indian Universities, that he fully believes in the reality of the powers ascribed to Yoga. It does not follow that he will at once say "Yes" to a European asking the question. He will probably say just the reverse from the apprehension I have spoken of above, but push your questions home and, you will discover the truth, as I did, for example, in the case of a very intelligent English-speaking native vakeel in an influential position and in constant relations with high European officials, last year. At first my new acquaintance met my inquiries as to whether he knew anything about these subjects with a wooden look of complete ignorance, and an explicit denial of any knowledge as to what I meant at all. It was not till the second time I saw him in private, at my own house, that by degrees it grew upon him that I was in earnest, and knew something about Yoga myself, and then he quietly opened out his real thoughts on the subject, and showed me that he knew not only perfectly well what I meant all along, but was stocked with information concerning occurrences and phenomena of an occult or apparently supernatural order, many of which had been observed in his own family and some by himself.

The point of all this is that Europeans are not justified in attributing to the jealousy of the occultists the absolute and entire ignorance of all that concerns them which pervades the modern society of the West. The West has been occupied with the business of material progress to the exclusion of psychological development. Perhaps it has done best for the world in confining itself to its specially; but however this may be, it has only itself to blame if its concentration of purpose has led to something like retrogression in another branch of development.

Jacolliot, a French writer, who has dealt at great length with various phases of Spiritism in the East, was told by one who must have been an adept to judge by the language used: "You have studied physical Nature, and you have obtained through the laws of Nature marvellous results—steam, electricity, etc., etc. For twenty-thousand years or more we have studied the intellectual forces; we have discovered their laws, and we obtain, by making them act alone or in concert with matter, phenomena still more astonishing than your own." Jacolliot adds: "We have seen things such as one does not describe for fear of making his readers doubt his intelligence......... but still we have seen them."

III

Occult phenomena must not be confused with the phenomena of spiritualism. The latter, whatever they may be, are manifestations which mediums can neither control nor understand in a scientific sense. The former are achievements of a conscious, living operator comprehending the laws with which he works. If these achievements appear miraculous, that is the fault of the observer's ignorance. The spiritualist knows perfectly well, in spite of ignorant mockery on the part of outsiders content to laugh without knowing what they are laughing at, that all kinds of occurrences distinctly outside the range of physical causation do constantly take place for inquirers who hunt them with sufficient diligence. But he has never been able to do more than frame hypotheses in respect to the hidden laws of Nature by virtue of which they have been produced. He has taken up a certain hypothesis *faute de mieux* in the first instance, and working always on this idea, has constructed such an elaborate edifice of theory round the facts that he is very reluctant to tolerate the interposition of a new hypothesis which will oblige him to revise his conclusions in some very important particulars. There will be no way of avoiding this necessity, however, if he belongs to the order of inquirers who care rather to be sure they have laid hold of the truth than to fortify a doctrine they have espoused for better or for worse.

Broadly speaking, there is scarcely one of the phenomena of spiritualism that adepts in occultism cannot reproduce by the force of their own will, supplemented by a comprehension of the resources of Nature. As will be seen when I come to a direct narrative of my own experiences, I have seen some of the most familiar phenomena of spiritualism produced by purely human agency. The old original spirit—rap which introduced the mightier phenomena of spiritualism has been manifested for my edification in a countless variety of ways, and under conditions which render the hypothesis of any spiritual agency in the matter wholly preposterous. I have seen flowers fall from the blank ceiling of a room under circumstances that gave me a practical assurance that no spiritual agency was at work, though in a manner as absolutely "supernatural" in the sense of being produced without the aid of any material appliances, as any of the floral showers by which some spiritual mediums are attended. I have over and over again received "direct writing," produced on paper in sealed envelopes of my own, which was created or precipitated by a living human correspondent. I have information, which, though second-hand, is very trustworthy, of a great variety of other familiar spiritual phenomena produced in the same way by human adepts in occultism. But it is not my present task to make war on spiritualism. The announcements I have to make will, indeed, be probably received more readily among spiritualists than in the outer circles of the ordinary world, for the spiritualists are at all events aware, from their own experience, that the orthodox science of the day does not know the last word concerning mind and matter, while the orthodox outsider stupidly clings to a denial of facts when these are of a nature which he foresees himself unable to explain. As the facts of spiritualism, though accessible to any honest man who goes in search of them, are not of a kind which anyone can carry about and fling in the faces of pragmatic "sceptics," these latter are enabled to keep up their professions of incredulity without the foolishness of their position being obvious to each other, plain as it is to "the initiated." However, although in this way the ordinary scientific mind will be reluctant to admit either the trustworthiness of my testimony or the conceivability of my explanations, it may allay some hostile prejudices to make clear at the onset that occult science deals with no guesswork concerning the post-mortem intervention of human beings in the affairs of this world. Its methods are as precise, and its mental discipline as rigid, as those of the laboratory or the university lecture-room. Wedding with theosophic research, spiritualism itself might guard itself from all those hasty inferences which have done so much to turn large sections of the cultivated people against it, and if they will but take the trouble to approach the subject from the point of view of occult science, students of physical Nature will be enabled at last to handle the *phenomena* of spiritualism freely, to consider them apart from the theories to which they have prematurely given rise; and thus relieved of the repugnance they feel for them at present, to bring them within the area of that which they at last will willingly recognise as true scientific generalisations.

OCCULTISM AND THE ADEPTS

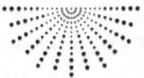

I

THE POWERS with which occultism invests its adepts include, to begin with, a control over various forces in Nature which ordinary science knows nothing about, and by means of which an adept can hold conversation with any other adept, whatever intervals on the earth's surface may lie between them. This psychological telegraphy is wholly independent of all mechanical conditions or appliances whatever. And the clairvoyant faculties of the adept are so perfect and complete that they amount to a species of omniscience as regards mundane affairs. The body is the prison of the soul for ordinary mortals. We can see merely what comes before its windows; we can take cognisance only of what is brought within its bars. But the adept has found the key of his prison and can emerge from it at pleasure. It is no longer a prison for him—merely a dwelling. In other words, the adept can project his soul out of his body to any place he pleases with the rapidity of thought.

The whole edifice of occultism from basement to roof is so utterly strange to ordinary conceptions that it is difficult to know how to begin an explanation of its contents. How could one describe a calculating machine to an audience unfamiliar with the simplest mechanical contrivances and knowing nothing of arithmetic. And the highly cultured classes of modern Europe, as regards the achievements of occultism, are, in spite of the perfection of their literary scholarship and the exquisite precision of their attainments in their own departments of science, in the position as regards occultism of knowing nothing about the A B C of the subject, nothing about the capacities of the soul at all as distinguished from the capacities of body and soul combined. The occultists for ages have devoted themselves to that study chiefly; they have accomplished results in connexion with it which are absolutely bewildering in their magnificence; but suddenly introduced to some of these, the prosaic intelligence is staggered and feels in a world of miracle and enchantment. On charts that show the stream of history, the nations all intermingle more or less, except the Chinese, and that is shown coming down in a single river without affluents and without branches from out of the clouds of time. Suppose that civilized Europe had not come into contact with the Chinese till lately, and suppose that the Chinamen, very much brighter in intelligence than they really are, had developed some branch of physical science to the point it actually has reached with us; suppose that particular branch had been entirely neglected with us, the surprise we should feel at taking up the Chinese discoveries in their refined development without having gradually grown familiar with their small beginnings would be very great. Now this is exactly the situation as regards occult science. The occultists have been a race apart from an earlier period than we can fathom—not a separate race physically, not a uniform race physically at all, nor a nation in any sense of the word, but a continuous association of men of the highest intelligence linked together by a bond stronger than any other tie of which mankind has experience, and carrying on with a perfect continuity of purpose the studies and traditions and mysteries of self-development handed down to them by their predecessors. All this time the stream of civilization, on the foremost waves of which the culture of modern Europe is floating, has been wholly and absolutely neglectful of the one study with which the occultists have been solely engaged. What wonder that the two lines of civilization have diverged so far apart that their forms are now entirely unlike each other. It remains to be seen whether this attempt to reintroduce the long—estranged cousins will be tolerated or treated as an impudent attempt to pass off an impostor as a relation.

I have said that the occultist can project his soul from his body. As an incidental discovery, it will be observed, he has thus ascertained beyond all shadow of doubt that he really has got a soul. A comparison of myths has sometimes been called the science of religion. If there can really be a science of religion it must necessarily be occultism. On the surface, perhaps, it may not be obvious that religious truth must necessarily open out more completely to the soul as temporarily loosened from the body, than to the soul as taking cognisance of ideas through the medium of the physical senses. But to ascend into a realm of immateriality, where cognition becomes a process of pure perception while the intellectual faculties are in full play and centred in the immaterial man, must manifestly be conducive to an enlarged comprehension of religious truth.

I have just spoken of the "immaterial man" as distinguished from the body of the physical senses; but, so complex is the statement I have to make, that I must no sooner induce the reader to tolerate the phrase than I must reject it for the future as inaccurate. Occult philosophy has ascertained that the inner ethereal self, which is the man as distinguished from his body, is itself the envelope of something more ethereal still—is itself, in a subtle sense of the term, material.

The majority of civilized people believe that man has a soul which will somehow survive the dissolution of the body; but they have to confess that they do not *know* very much about it. A good many of the most highly civilized, have grave doubts on the subject, and some think that researches in physics which have suggested the notion that even thought may be a mode of motion, tend to establish the strong probability of the hypothesis that when the life of the body is destroyed nothing else survives. Occult philosophy does not speculate about the matter at all; it knows the state of the facts.

St. Paul, who was an occultist, speaks of man as constituted of body, soul, and spirit. The distinction is one that hardly fits in with the theory, that when a man dies his soul is translated to heaven or hell for ever. What then becomes of the spirit, and what is the spirit as different from the soul, on the ordinary hypothesis. Orthodox thinkers work out each some theory on the subject for himself. Either that the soul is the seat of the emotions and the spirit of the intellectual faculties, or *vice versa*. No one can put such conjectures on a solid foundation, not even on the basis of an alleged revelation. But St. Paul was not indulging in vague fancies when he made use of the expression quoted. The spirit he was referring to may be described as the soul of the soul. With that for the moment we need not be concerned. The important point which occultism brings out is that the soul of man, while something enormously subtler and more ethereal and more lasting than the body, is itself a *material* reality. Not material as chemistry understands matter, but as physical science en *bloc* might understand it if the tentacle of each branch of science were to grow more sensitive and were to work more in harmony. It is no denial of the materiality of any hypothetical substance to say that one cannot determine its atomic weight and its affinities. The ether that transmits light is held to be material by anyone who holds it to exist at all, but there is a gulf of difference between it and the thinnest of the gases. You do not always approach a scientific truth from the same direction. You may perceive some directly; you have to infer others indirectly; but these latter may not on that account be the less certain. The materiality of ether is inferable from the behaviour of light: the materiality of the soul may be inferable from its subjection to forces. A mesmeric influence is a force emanating from certain physical characteristics of the mesmerist. It impinges on the soul of the subject at a distance and produces an effect perceptible to him, demonstrable to others. Of course this is an illustration and no proof. I must set forth as well as I am able—and that can but be very imperfectly—the discoveries of occultism without at first attempting the establishment by proof of each part of these discoveries. Further on, I shall be able to prove some parts at any rate, and others will then be recognised as indirectly established, too.

The soul is material, and inheres in the ordinarily more grossly material body; and it is this condition of things which enables the occultist to speak positively on the subject, for he can satisfy himself at one coup that there is such a thing as a soul, and that it is material in its nature, by dissociating it from the body under some conditions, and restoring it again. The occultist can even do this sometimes with other souls; his primary achievement, however, is to do so with his own. When I say that the occultist *knows* he has a soul I refer to this power. He knows it just as another man knows he has a great coat. He can put it from him, and render it manifest as something separate from himself. But remember that to him, when the separation is effected, he *is* the soul and the thing put off is the body. And this is to attain nothing less than absolute certainty about the great problem of survival after death. The adept does not rely on faith, or on metaphysical speculation, in regard to the possibilities of his existence apart from the body. He experiences such an existence whenever he pleases, and although it may be allowed that the more art of emancipating himself temporarily from the body would not necessarily inform him concerning his ultimate destinies after that emancipation should be final at death, it gives him, at all events, exact knowledge concerning the conditions under which he will start on his journey in the next world. While his body lives, his soul is, so to speak, a captive balloon (though with a very long, elastic and imponderable cable). Captive ascents will not necessarily tell him whether the balloon will float when at last the machinery below breaks up, and he finds himself altogether adrift; but it is something to be an aeronaut already, before the journey begins, and to know definitely, as I said before, that there are such things as balloons, for certain emergencies, to sail in.

There would be infinite grandeur in the faculty I have described alone, supposing that were the end of adeptship; but instead of being the end, it is more like the beginning. The seemingly magic feats which the adepts in occultism have the power to perform, are accomplished, I am given to understand, by means of familiarity with a force in nature which is referred to in Sanskrit writings as *akas*. Western science has done much in discovering some of the properties and powers of electricity. Occult science, ages before, had done much more in discovering the properties and powers of *akas*. In "The Coming Race," the late Lord Bulwer Lytton, whose connexion with occultism appears to have been closer than the world generally has yet realised, gives a fantastic and imaginative account of the wonders achieved in the world to which his hero penetrates, by means of Vril. In writing of Vril, Lord Lytton has clearly been poetising *akas*. "The Coming Race" is described as a people entirely unlike adepts in many essential particulars—as a complete nation, for one thing, of men and women all equally handling the powers, even from childhood, which—or some of which among others not described—the adepts have conquered. This is a mere fairytale, founded on the achievements of occultism. But no one who has made a study of the latter can fail to see, can fail to recognise with a conviction amounting to certainty, that the author of "The Coming Race" must have been familiar with the leading ideas of occultism, perhaps with a great deal more. The same evidence is afforded by Lord Lytton's other novels of mystery, "Zanoni," and "The Strange Story." In "Zanoni," the sublime personage in the background, Mejnour, is intended plainly to be a great adept of Eastern occultism, exactly like those of whom I have to speak. It is difficult to know why in this case, where Lord Lytton has manifestly intended to adhere much more closely to the real facts of occultism than in "The Coming Race," he should have represented Mejnour as a solitary survivor of the Rosicrucian fraternity. The guardians of occult science are content to be a small body as compared with the tremendous importance of the knowledge which they save from perishing, but they have never allowed their numbers to diminish to the extent of being in any danger of ceasing to exist as an organised body on earth. It is difficult again to understand why Lord Lytton, having learned so much as he certainly did, should have been content to use up his information merely as an ornament of fiction, instead of giving it to the world in a form which should claim more serious consideration. At all events, prosaic people will argue to that effect; but it is not impossible that Lord Lytton himself had become, through long study of the subject, so permeated with the love of mystery which inheres in the occult mind apparently, that he preferred to throw out his information in a veiled and mystic shape, so that it would be intelligible to readers in sympathy with himself, and would blow unnoticed past the commonplace understanding without awakening the angry rejection which these pages, for example, if they are destined to attract any notice at all, will assuredly encounter at the hands of bigots in science, religion, and the great philosophy of the commonplace.

Akas, be it then understood, is a force for which we have no name, and in reference to which we have no experience to guide us to a conception of its nature. One can only grasp at the idea required by conceiving that it is as much more potent, subtle, and extraordinary an agent than electricity, as electricity is superior in subtlety and variegated efficiency to steam. It is through his acquaintance with the properties of this force, that the adept can accomplish the physical phenomena, which I shall presently be able to show are within his reach, besides others of far greater magnificence.

II

Who are the adepts who handle the tremendous forces of which I speak? There is reason to believe that such adepts have existed in all historic ages, and there are such adepts in India at this moment, or in adjacent countries. The identity of the knowledge they have inherited, with that of ancient initiates in occultism, follows irresistibly from an examination of the views they hold and the faculties they exercise. The conclusion has to be worked out from a mass of literary evidence, and it will be enough to state it for the moment, pointing out the proper channels of research in the matter afterwards. For the present let us consider the position of the adepts as they now exist, or, to use the designation more generally employed in India, of "the Mahatmas." [1]

They constitute a Brotherhood, or Secret Association, which ramifies all over the East, but the principal seat of which for the present I gather to be in Tibet. But India has not yet been deserted by the adepts, and from that country they still receive many recruits. For the great fraternity is at once the least and the most exclusive organization in the world, and fresh recruits from any race or country are welcome, provided they possess the needed qualifications. The door, as I have been told by one who is himself an adept, is always open to the right man who knocks, but the road that has to be travelled before the door is reached is one which none but very determined travellers can hope to pass. It is manifestly impossible that I can describe its perils in any but very general terms, but it is not necessary to have learned any secrets of initiation to understand the character of the training through which a neophyte must pass before he attains the dignity of a proficient in occultism. The adept is not made: he becomes, as I have been constantly assured, and the process of becoming is mainly in his own hands.

Never, I believe, in less than seven years from the time at which a candidate for initiation is accepted as a probationer, is he ever admitted to the very first of the ordeals, whatever they may be, which bar the way to the earliest decrees of occultism, and there is no security for him that the seven years may not be extended *ad libitum*. He has no security that he will ever be admitted to any initiation whatever. Nor is this appalling uncertainty, which would alone deter most Europeans, however keen upon the subject intellectually, from attempting to advance, themselves, into the domain of occultism, maintained from the mere caprice of a despotic society, coquetting, so to speak, with the eagerness of its wooers. The trials through which the neophyte has to pass are no fantastic mockeries, or mimicries of awful peril. Nor, do I take it, are they artificial barriers set up by the masters of occultism, to try the nerve of their pupils, as a riding—master might put up fences in his school. It is inherent in the nature of the science that has to be explored, that its revelations shall stagger the reason and try the most resolute courage. It is in his own interest that the candidate's character and fixity of purpose, and perhaps his physical and mental attributes, are tested and watched with infinite care and patience in the first instance, before he is allowed to take the final plunge into the sea of strange experiences through which he must swim with the strength of his own right arm, or perish.

As to what may be the nature of the trials that await him during the period of his development, it will be obvious that I can have no accurate knowledge, and conjectures based on fragmentary revelations pictured up here and there are not worth recording, but as for the nature of the life led by the mere candidate for admission as a neophyte it will be equally plain that no secret is involved. The ultimate development of the adept requires amongst other things a life of absolute physical purity, and the candidate must, from the beginning, give practical evidence of his willingness to adopt this. He must, that is to say, for all the years of his probation, be perfectly chaste, perfectly abstemious, and indifferent to physical luxury of every sort. This regimen does not involve any fantastic discipline or obtrusive asceticism, nor withdrawal from the world. There would be nothing to prevent a gentleman in ordinary society from being in some of the preliminary stages of training for occult candidature without anybody about him being the wiser. For true occultism, the sublime achievement of the real adept, is not attained through the loathsome asceticism of the ordinary Indian fakir, the *yogi* of the woods and wilds, whose dirt accumulates with his sanctity—of the fanatic who fastens iron hooks into his flesh, or holds up an arm until it is withered. An imperfect knowledge of some of the external facts of Indian occultism will often lead to a misunderstanding on this point. *Yog Vidya* is the Indian name for occult science, and it is easy to learn a good deal more than is worth learning about the practices of some misguided enthusiasts who cultivate some of its inferior branches by means of mere physical exercises. Properly speaking, this physical development is called *Hatti Yog*, while the loftier sort, which is approached by the discipline of the mind, and which leads to the high altitudes of occultism, is called *Ragi yog*. No person whom a real occultist would ever think of as an adept, has acquired his powers by means of the laborious and puerile exercises of the *Hatti yog*. I do not mean to say that these inferior exercises are altogether futile. They do invest the person who pursues them with some abnormal faculties and powers. Many treatises have been written to describe them, and many people who have lived in India will be able to relate curious experiences they have had with proficients in this extraordinary craft. I do not wish to fill these pages with tales of wonder that I have had no means of sifting, or it would be easy to collect examples; but the point to insist on here is that no story anyone can have heard or read which seems to put an ignoble, or petty, or low-minded aspect on Indian *yogeeism* can have any application to the ethereal *yogeeism* which is called *Ragi yog*, and which leads to the awful heights of true adeptship.

---

1. Mahatma—Great Soul, or Great Spirit, derived from *Maha* and *Atma*.

THE THEOSOPHICAL SOCIETY

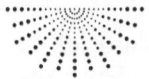

SECRET as the occult organization has always remained, there is a good deal more to be learned concerning the philosophical views which it has preserved or acquired, than might be supposed at the first glance. As my own experience when fully described will show, the great adepts of occultism themselves have no repugnance to the dissemination of their religions philosophy So far as a world untrained as ours is in pure psychological investigation can profit by such teaching. Nor even are they unconquerably averse to the occasional manifestation of those superior powers over the forces of Nature to which their extraordinary researches have led them. The many apparently miraculous phenomena which I have witnessed through occult agency could never have been exhibited if the general rule which precludes the Brothers from the exhibition of their powers to uninitiated persons were absolute. As a general rule, indeed, the display of any occult phenomenon for the purpose of exciting the wonder and admiration of beholders is strictly forbidden. And indeed I should imagine that such prohibition is absolute if there is no higher purpose involved. But it is plain that with a purely philanthropic desire to spread the credit of a philosophical system which is ennobling in its character, the Brothers may sometimes wisely permit the display of abnormal phenomena when the minds to which such an appeal t is made may be likely to rise from the appreciation of the wonder to a befitting respect for the philosophy in which it accredits. And the history of the Theosophical Society has been an expansion of this idea.

That history has been a chequered one, because the phenomena that have been displayed have often failed of their effect, have sometimes become the subject of a premature publicity, and have brought down on the study of occult philosophy as regarded from the point of view of the outer world, and on the devoted persons who have been chiefly identified with its encouragement by means of the Theosophical Society, a great deal of stupid ridicule and some malevolent persecution. It may be asked why the Brothers, if they are really the great and all-powerful persons I represent them, have permitted indiscretions of the kind referred to, but the inquiry is not so embarrassing as it may seem at the first glance. If the picture of the Brothers that I have endeavoured to present to the reader has been appreciated rightly, it will show them less accurately qualified, in spite of their powers, than persons of lesser occult development, to carry on any undertaking which involves direct relations with a multiplicity of ordinary people in the commonplace world. I gather the primary purpose of the Brotherhood to be something very unlike the task I am engaged in, for example, at this moment—the endeavour to convince the public generally that there really are faculties latent in humanity capable of such extraordinary development, that they carry us at a bound to an immense distance beyond the dreams of physical science in reference to the comprehension of Nature, and at the same time afford us positive testimony concerning the constitution and destinies of the human soul. That is a task on which it is reasonable to suppose the Brothers would cast a sympathetic glance, but it will be obvious on a moment's reflection, that their primary duty must be to keep alive the actuality of that knowledge, and of those powers concerning which I am merely giving some shadowy account. If the Brothers were to employ themselves on the large, rough business of hacking away at the incredulity of a stolid multitude, at the acrimonious incredulity of the materialistic phalanx, at the terrified and indignant incredulity of the orthodox religious world, it is conceivable that they might—*propter vitam vivendi perdere causas*—suffer the occult science itself to decay for the sake of persuading mankind that it did really exist. Of course it might be suggested that division of labour might be possible in occultism as in everything else, and that some adepts qualified for the work might be told off for the purpose of breaking down the incredulity of modern science, while the others would carry on the primary duties of their career in their own beloved seclusion. But a suggestion of this kind, however practical it may sound to a practical world, would probably present itself as eminently unpractical to the true mystic. To begin with, an aspirant for occult honours does not go through the tremendous and prolonged effort required to win him success, in order at the end of all things to embrace a life in the midst of the ordinary world, which on the hypothesis of his success in occultism must necessarily be repugnant to him in the extreme.

Probably there is not one real adept who does not look with greater aversion and repugnance on any life *except* a life of seclusion, than we of the outer world would look on the notion of being buried alive in a remote mountain fastness where no foot or voice from the outer world could penetrate. I shall very soon be able to show that the love of seclusion, inherent in adeptship, does not imply a mind vacant of the knowledge of European culture and manners. It is, on the contrary, compatible with an amount of European culture and experience that people acquainted merely with the commonplace aspects of Eastern life will be surprised to find possible in the case of a man of Oriental birth. Now, the imaginary adept told off of the suggestion I am examining, to show the scientific world that there are realms of knowledge it has not yet explored and faculties attainable to man that it has not yet dreamed of possessing, would have to be either appointed to discharge that duty, or to volunteer for it. In the one case we have to assume that the occult fraternity is despotic in its treatment of its members in a manner which all my observation leads me to believe it certainly is not; in the other, we have to suppose some adept making a voluntary sacrifice of what he regards as not only the most agreeable but also the higher life—for what? for the sake of accomplishing a task which he does not regard as of very great importance—relatively, at any rate, to that other task in which he may take a part—the perpetuation and perhaps the development of the great science itself. But I do not care to follow the argument any further, because it will come on for special treatment in a different way presently. Enough for the moment to indicate that there are considerations against the adoption of that method of persuasion which, as far as the judgment of ordinary people would go, would seem the best suited to the introduction of occult truths to modern intelligence.

And these considerations appear to have prompted the acceptance by the Brothers, of the Theosophical Society as a more or less imperfect, but still the best available agency for the performance of a piece of work, in which, without being actually prepared to enter on it themselves, they nevertheless take a cordial interest.

And what are the peculiar conditions which render the Theosophical Society, the organization and management of which have been faulty in many ways, the best agency hitherto available for the propagation of occult truths? The zeal and qualifications of its founder, Madame Blavatsky, give the explanation required. It is obvious that to give any countenance or support at all to a society concerned with the promulgation of occult philosophy, it was necessary for the Brothers to be in occult communication with it in some way or other. For it must be remembered that though it may seem to us a very amazing and impossible thing to sit still at home and impress our thoughts upon the mind of a distant friend by an effort of will, a Brother living in an unknown Himalayan retreat is not only able to converse as freely as he likes with any of his friends who are initiates like himself, in whatever part of the world they may happen to be, but would find any other modes of communication, such as those with which the crawling faculties of the outer world have to be content, simply intolerable in their tedium and inefficacy. Besides, he must be able to afford assistance to any society having its sphere of operations among people in the world, be able to hear from it with the same facility that he can send communications to it. So there must be an initiate at the other end of the line Finally, the occult rules evidently require this last-named condition, or what amounts to the same thing, forbid arrangements which can only be avoided on this condition.

Now, Madame Blavatsky is an initiate—is an adept to the extent of possessing this magnificent power of psychological telegraphy with her occult friends. That she has stopped short of that further development in adeptship that would have tided her right over the boundary between this and the occult world altogether, is the circumstance which has rendered her assumption of the task with which the Theosophical Society is concerned compatible with the considerations pointed out above as operating to prevent the assumption of such a duty by a full adept. As regards the supremely essential characteristic, she has, in fact, been exactly suited to the emergency. How it came to pass that her occult training carried her as far as it did and no further, is a question into which it is fruitless to inquire, because the answer would manifestly entail explanations which would impinge too closely on the secrets of initiation which are never disclosed under any circumstances whatever. After all she is a woman—though her powerful mind, widely if erratically cultivated, and perfectly dauntless courage proved among other ways on the battlefield, but more than by any bravery with bullets, by her occult initiation, renders the name, connoting what I it ordinarily does, rather absurd in application to her—and this has, perhaps, barred her from the highest degrees in occultism that she might otherwise have attained. At all events, after a course of occult study carried on for seven years in a Himalayan retreat, and crowning a devotion to occult pursuits extending over five-and-thirty or forty years, Madame Blavatsky reappeared in the world, dazed, as she met ordinary people going about in commonplace, benighted ignorance concerning the wonders of occult science, at the mere thought of the stupendous gulf of experience that separated her from them. She could hardly at first bear to associate with them, for thinking of all she knew that they did not know and that she was bound not to reveal. Any one can understand the burden of a great secret, but the burden of such a secret as occultism, and the burden of great powers only conferred on condition that their exercise should be very strictly circumscribed by rule, must have been trying indeed.

Circumstances—or to put the matter more plainly, the guidance of friends from whom, though she had left them behind in the Himalayas on her return to Europe, she was no longer in danger of separation, as we understand the term, induced her to visit America, and there, assisted by some other persons whose interest in the subject was kindled by occasional manifestations of her extraordinary powers, and notably by Colonel Olcott, its life-devoted President, she founded the Theosophical Society, the objects of which, as originally defined, were to explore the latent psychological powers of man, and the ancient Oriental literature in which the clue to these may be hidden, and in which the philosophy of occult science may be partly discovered.

The Society took root readily in America, while branches were also formed in England and elsewhere; but, leaving these to take care of themselves, Madame Blavatsky ultimately returned to India, to establish the Society there among the natives, from whose natural hereditary sympathies with mysticism it was reasonable to expect an ardent sympathy with a psychological enterprise which not only appealed to their intuitive belief in the reality of *yog vidya*, but also to their best patriotism, by exhibiting India as the fountainhead of the highest if the least known and the most secluded culture in the world.

Here, however, began the practical blunders in the management of the Theosophical Society which led to the incidents referred to above, as having given it, so far, a chequered career. Madame Blavatsky, to begin with, was wholly unfamiliar with the everyday side of Indian life, her previous visits having brought her only into contact with groups of people utterly unconnected with the current social system and characteristics of the country Nor could she have undertaken a worse preparation for Indian life than that supplied by a residence of some years in the United States. This sent her out to India unfurnished with the recommendations which she could readily have obtained, if she had spent the time just referred to in England, and left her unprovided with information it was highly important for her to possess concerning the true character of the British ruling classes of India and their relations with the people.

The consequence was that Mme. Blavatsky, on her first arrival in India, adopted an attitude of obtrusive sympathy with the natives of the soil as compared with the Europeans, seeking their society in a manner which, coupled with the fact that she made none of the usual advances to European society, and with her manifestly Russian name, had the effect not unnaturally of rendering her *suspecte* to the rather clumsy organization which in India attempts to combine with sundry others, the functions of a political police. These suspicions, it is true, were allayed almost as soon as they were conceived, but not before Madame Blavatsky had been made for a short time the object of an *espionage* so awkward that it became grossly obvious to herself and roused her indignation to fever heat. To a more phlegmatic nature the incident would have been little more than amusing, but all accidents combined to develop trouble. A Russian by birth, though naturalised in the United States, Madame Blavatsky is probably more sensitive than an English woman, less experienced in political espionage would be to the insult involved in being taken for a spy. Then the inner consciousness of having, for enthusiasm in the purely intellectual or spiritual enterprise to which she had devoted her life, renounced the place in society to which her distinguished birth and family naturally entitled her, probably intensified the bitterness of her indignation, at finding the sacrifice not only unappreciated, but turned against her, and regarded as justifying a foul suspicion. At all events, the circumstances acting on an excitable temperament led her to make public protests which caused it to be widely known by natives as well as by Europeans, that she had been looked at askance by Government authorities. And this idea for a time impeded the success of her work. Nothing can be done in India without a European impulse in the beginning; at all events, it handicaps any enterprise frightfully to be without such an impulse if native co-operation is required. Not that the Theosophical Society failed to get members. The natives were flattered at the attitude towards them taken up by their new "European" friends, as Madame Blavatsky and Colonel Olcott were no doubt generally regarded in spite of their American nationality, and showed a shallow eagerness to become Theosophists. But their ardour did not always prove durable, and in some few cases they showed a lamentable want of earnestness by breaking away from the Society altogether.

Meanwhile, Madame Blavatsky began to make friends amongst the Europeans, and in 1880 visited Simla, where she began late in the day to approach her work from the right direction. Again, however, some mistakes were made which have retarded the establishment of the Theosophical Society, as far as India is concerned, on the dignified footing that it ought to occupy. A great many wonderful phenomena were manifested in the presence at various times of a great many people; but proper safeguards were not taken to avert the great danger that must always attend such a method of recommending occult science to public notice. It is beyond dispute that phenomena, exhibited under thoroughly satisfactory conditions to persons intelligent enough to comprehend their significance, create an effect in awakening a thirst for the study of occult philosophy that no other appeal can produce. But it is equally true, though at the first glance this may not be so apparent, that to minds, quite unprepared by previous training to grasp the operation of occult forces, the most perfectly unimpeachable phenomenon will be received rather as an insult to the understanding than as a proof of the operation of occult power. This is especially the case with persons of merely average intelligence, of whose faculties cannot stand the shock of a sudden appeal to an entirely new set of ideas. The strain is too great; the new chain of reasoning breaks, and the commonplace observer of abnormal occurrences reverts to his original frame of stolid incredulity, perfectly unaware of the fact that a revelation of priceless intellectual importance has been offered to him and has been misunderstood. Nothing is commoner than to hear people say: "I can't believe in the reality of a phenomenal occurrence unless I see it for myself. Show it me and I shall believe in it, but not till then." Many people who say this are quite mistaken as to what they would believe if the occurrence were shown to them. I have over and over again seen phenomena of an absolutely genuine nature pass before the eyes of people unused to investigating occurrences of the kind, and leave no impression behind beyond an irritated conviction that they were somehow being taken in. Just this happened in some conspicuous instances at Simla, and it is needless to say that many as were the phenomena that Madame Blavatsky produced, or was instrumental in producing, during the visit to which I am referring, the number of people in the place who had no opportunity of seeing them was considerably greater than that of the witnesses. And for these, as a rule, the whole series of incidents presented itself simply as an imposition. It was nothing to the purpose for the holders of this theory that there was a glaring absence from the whole business of any motive for imposture, that a considerable group of persons whose testimony and capacity would never have been impugned had any other matter been under discussion, were emphatic in their declarations as to the complete reality of the phenomena that had been displayed. The commonplace mind could not assimilate the idea that it was face to face with a new revelation in Nature, and any hypothesis, no matter how absurd and illogical in its details, was preferable for the majority to the simple grandeur of the truth.

On the whole, therefore, as Madame Blavatsky became a celebrity in India, her relations with European society were intensified. She made many friends, and secured some ardent converts to a belief in the reality of occult powers; but she became the innocent object of bitter animosity on the part of some other acquaintances, who, unable to assimilate what they saw in her presence, took up all attitude of disbelief, which deepened into positive enmity as the whole subject became enveloped in a cloud of more or less excited controversy.

And it is needless to say that many of the newspapers made great capital out of the whole situation ridiculing Madame Blavatsky's dupes, and twisting every bit of information that came out about her phenomena into the most ludicrous shape it could be made to assume. Mockery of that sort was naturally expected by English friends who avowed their belief in the reality of Madame Blavatsky's powers, and probably never gave one of them a moment's serious annoyance. But for the oversensitive and excitable person chiefly concerned they were indescribably tormenting, and eventually it grew doubtful whether her patience would stand the strain put upon it; whether she would not relinquish altogether the ungrateful task of inducing the world at large to accept the good gifts, which she had devoted her life to offering them. Happily, so far, no catastrophe has ensued; but no history of Columbus in chains for discovering a new world, or Galileo in prison for announcing the true principles of astronomy, is more remarkable for those who know all the bearings of the situation in India, as regards the Theosophical Society, than the sight of Madam Blavatsky, slandered and ridiculed by most of the Anglo-Indian papers, and spoken of as a charlatan by the commonplace crowd, in return for having freely offered them some of the wonderful fruits—as much as the rules of the great occult association permit her to offer—of the life-long struggle in which she has conquered her extraordinary knowledge.

In spite of all this, meanwhile, the Theosophical Society remains the one organization which supplies to inquirers who thirst for occult knowledge a link of communication, however slight, with the great fraternity in the background which takes an interest in its progress, and is accessible to its founder.

FIRST OCCULT EXPERIENCES

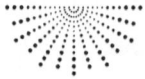

IT HAS BEEN through my connection with the Theosophical Society and my acquaintance with Madame Blavatsky that I have obtained experiences in connection with occultism, which have prompted me to undertake my present task. The first problem I had to solve was whether Madame Blavatsky really did, as I heard, possess the power of producing abnormal phenomena. And it may be imagined that, on the assumption of the reality of her phenomena, nothing would have been simpler than to obtain such satisfaction when once I had formed her acquaintance. It is, however, an illustration of the embarrassments which surround all inquiries of this nature—embarrassments with which so many people grow impatient, to the end that they cast inquiry altogether aside and remain wholly ignorant of the truth for the rest of their lives—that although on the first occasion of my making. Madame Blavatsky's acquaintance she became a guest at my house at Allahabad and remained there for six weeks, the harvest of satisfaction I was enabled to obtain during this time was exceedingly small. Of course I heard a great deal from her during the time mentioned about occultism and the Brothers, but while she was most anxious that I should understand the situation thoroughly, and I was most anxious to get at the truth, the difficulties to be overcome were almost insuperable. For the Brothers, as already described, have an unconquerable objection to showing off. That the person who wishes them to show off is an earnest seeker of truth, and not governed by mere idle curiosity, is nothing to the purpose. They do not want to attract candidates for initiation by an exhibition of wonders. Wonders have a very spirit-stirring effect on the history of every religion founded on miracles, but occultism is not a pursuit which people can safely take up in obedience to the impulse of enthusiasm created by witnessing a display of extraordinary power. There is no absolute rule to forbid the exhibition of powers in presence of the outsider; but it is clearly disapproved of by the higher authorities of occultism on principle, and it is practically impossible for less exalted proficients to go against this disapproval. It was only the very slightest of all imaginable phenomena that, during her first visit to my house, Madame Blavatsky was thus permitted to exhibit freely. She was allowed to show that "raps" like those which spiritualists attribute to spirit agency, could be produced at will. This was something, and *faute de mieux* we paid great attention to raps.

Spiritualists are aware that when groups of people sit round a table and put their hands upon it, they will, if a "medium" be present, generally hear little knocks which respond to questions and spell out messages. The large outer circle of persons who do not believe in spiritualism are fain to imagine that all the millions who do, are duped as regards this impression. It must sometimes be troublesome for them to account for the wide development of the delusion, but any theory, they think, is preferable to admitting the possibility that the spirits of deceased persons can communicate in this way; or, if they take the scientific view of the matter, that a physical effect, however slight, can be produced without a physical cause. Such persons ought to welcome the explanations I am now giving, tending as these do to show that the theory of universal self-deception as regards spirit-rapping, which must be rather an awkward theory for anyone but a ludicrously conceited objector to hold, is not the only one by means of which the asserted facts of spiritualism—those with which we are now dealing at all events—can be reconciled with a reluctance to accept the spiritual hypothesis as the explanation.

Now, I soon found out not only that raps would always come at a table at which Madame Blavatsky sat with the view of obtaining such results, but that all conceivable hypotheses of fraud in the matter were rapidly disposed of by a comparison of the various experiments we were able to make. To begin with, there was no necessity for other people to sit at the table at all. We could work with any table under any circumstances, or without a table at all. A windowpane would do equally well, or the wall, or any door, or anything whatever which could give out a sound if hit. A half glass door put ajar was at once seen to be a very good instrument to choose, because it was easy to stand opposite Madame Blavatsky in this case, to see her bare hands or hand (without any rings) resting motionless on the pane, and to hear the little ticks come plainly, as if made with the point of a pencil or, with the sound of electric sparks passing from one knob of an electrical apparatus to another. Another very satisfactory way of obtaining the raps—one frequently employed in the evening—was to set down a large glass clock-shade on the hearthrug, and get Madame Blavatsky, after removing all rings from her hands, and sitting well clear of the shade so that no part of her dress touched it, to lay her hands on it. Putting a lamp on the ground opposite, and sitting down on the hearthrug, one could see the under surfaces of the hands resting on the glass, and still under these perfectly satisfactory conditions the raps would come, clear and distinct, on the sonorous surface of the shade.

It was out of Madame Blavatsky's power to give an exact explanation as to how these raps were produced. Every effort of occult power is connected with some secret or other, and slight, regarded in the light of phenomena, as the raps were, they were physical effects produced by an effort of will, and the manner in which the will can be trained to produce physical effects may be too uniform, as regards great and small phenomena, to be made in accordance with the rules of occultism the subject of exact explanations to uninitiated persons. But the fact that the raps were obedient to the will was readily put beyond dispute, in this way amongst others: working with the windowpane or the clock-shade, I would ask to have a name spelled out, mentioning one at random. Then I would call over the alphabet, and at the right letters the raps would come. Or I would ask for a definite number of raps, and they would come. Or for series of raps in some defined rhythmical progression, and they would come. Nor was this all. Madame Blavatsky would sometimes put her hands, or one only, on someone else's head, and make the raps come, audibly to an attentive listener and perceptibly to the person touched, who would feel each little shock exactly as if he were taking sparks off the conductor of an electrical machine.

At a later stage of my inquiries I obtained raps under better circumstances again than these—namely, without contact between the object on which they were produced and Madame Blavatsky's hands at all. This was at Simla in the summer of last year (1880), but I may as well anticipate a little as far as the raps are concerned. At Simla Madame Blavatsky used to produce the raps on a little table set in the midst of an attentive group, with no one touching it at all. After starting it, or of charging it with some influence by resting her hands on it for a few moments, she would hold one about a foot above it and make mesmeric passes at it, at each of which the table would yield the familiar sound. Nor was this done only at our own house with our own tables. The same thing would be done at friends houses, to which Madame Blavatsky accompanied us. And a further development of the head experiment was this: It was found to be possible for several persons to feel the same rap simultaneously. Four or five persons used sometimes to put their hands in a pile, one on another on a table; then Madame Blavatsky would put hers on the top of the pile and cause a current, of whatever it is which produces the sound, to pass through the whole series of hands, felt by each simultaneously, and record itself in a rap on the table beneath. Anyone who has ever taken part in forming such a pile of hands must feel as to some of the hypotheses concerning the raps that have been put forward in the Indian papers by determined sceptics—hard-headed persons not to be taken in—to the effect that the raps are produced by Madame Blavatsky's thumbnails or by the cracking of some joint—that such hypotheses are rather idiotic.

Summing up the argument in language which I used in a letter written at the time, it stands as follows; "Madame Blavatsky puts her hands on a table and raps are heard on it. Some wiseacre suggests she does it with her thumbnails; she puts only one hand on the table; the raps comes still. Does she conceal any artifice under her hand? She lifts her hand from the table altogether, and merely holding it in the air above, the raps still come. Has she done anything to the table? She puts her hand on a windowpane, on a picture frame, on a dozen different places about the room in succession, and from each in turn come the mysterious raps. Is the house where she stays with her own particular friends about her prepared all over? She goes to half a dozen other houses at Simla and produces raps at them all. Do the raps really come from somewhere else than where they seem to come from—are they perhaps ventriloquism? She puts her hand on your head, and from the motionless fingers you feel something which resembles a minute series of electric shocks, and an attentive listener beside you will hear them producing little raps on your skull. Are you telling a lie when you say you feel the shocks? Half a dozen people put their hands one on top of the other in a pile on the table; Madame Blavatsky puts hers on the top of all, and each person feels the little throbs pass through, and hears them record themselves in faint raps on the table on which the pile of hands is resting. When a person has seen all these experiments many times, as I have, what impression do you think is made on his mind by a person who says. There is nothing in raps but conjuring—Maskelyne and Cooke can do them for £10 a night. Maskelyne and Cooke cannot do them for £10 a night nor for ten lakhs a night under the circumstances I describe."

The raps even as I heard them during the first visit that Madame Blavatsky paid us at Allahabad, gave me a complete assurance that she was in possession of some faculties of an abnormal character. And this assurance lent a credibility, that would not otherwise have belonged to them, to one or two phenomena of a different kind which also occurred at that time, the conditions of which wore not complete enough to make them worth recording here. But it was mortifying to approach no nearer to absolute certitude concerning the questions in which we were really interested—namely, whether there did indeed exist men with the wonderful powers ascribed to the adepts, and whether in this way it was possible for human creatures to obtain positive knowledge concerning the characteristics of their own spiritual nature. It must be remembered that Madame Blavatsky was preaching no specific doctrine on this subject. What she told us about the adepts and her own initiation was elicited by questions. Theosophy, in which she did seek to interest all her friends, did not proclaim any specific belief on the subject. It simply recommended the theory that humanity should be regarded as a Universal Brotherhood in which each person should study the truth as regards spiritual things, freed from the prepossessions of any specific religious dogma. But although her attitude, as regards the whole subject, put her under no moral obligation to prove the reality of occultism, her conversation and her book, "Isis Unveiled," disclosed a view of things which one naturally desired to explore further; and it was tantalising to feel that she could, and yet could not give us the final proofs we so much desired to have, that her occult training really had invested her with powers over material things of a kind which, if one could but feel sure they were actually in her possession, would utterly shatter the primary foundations of materialistic philosophy.

One conviction we felt had been fully attained. This was the conviction of her own good faith. It is disagreeable merely to recognise that this can be impugned; but this has been done in Indiana so recklessly and cruelly by people who take up an attitude of hostility to the views with which she is identified, that it would be affectation to pass the question by. On the other hand, it would be too great a concession to an ignoble attack to go minutely over the evidence of her honesty of character with which my intimacy with Madame Blavatsky has gradually supplied me. At various times she has been a guest of ours for periods now amounting in all to more than three months out of nearly two years. To any impartial intelligence it will be manifest that, under these circumstances, I must have been able to form a better opinion concerning her real character than can possibly be derived from the crude observations of persons who have perhaps met her once or twice. I am not, of course, attributing any scientific value to this sort of testimony as accrediting the abnormal character of phenomena she may be concerned in producing. With such a mighty problem at stake as the trustworthiness of the fundamental theories of modern physical science, it is impossible to proceed by any other but scientific modes of investigation. In any experiments I have tried I have always been careful to exclude, not merely the probability, but the possibility of trickery; and where it has been impossible to secure the proper conditions, I have not allowed the results of the experiment to enter into the sum total of my conclusions. But, in its place, it seems only right—only a slight attempt to redress the scandalous wrong which, as far as mere insult and slander can do a wrong, has been done to a very high-minded and perfectly honourable woman—to record the certainty at which in progress of time both my wife and myself arrived, that Madame Blavatsky is a lady of absolutely upright nature, who has sacrificed, not merely rank and fortune, but all thought of personal welfare or comfort in any shape, from enthusiasm for occult studies in the first instance, and latterly for the special task she has taken in hand as an initiate in, if relatively a humble member of, the great occult fraternity—the direction of the Theosophical Society.

Besides the production of the raps one other phenomenon had been conceded to us during Madame Blavatsky's first visit. We had gone with her to Benares for a few days, and were studying at a house lent to us by the Maharajah of Vizianagram—a big, bare, comfortless abode as judged by European standards—in the central hall of which we were sitting one evening after dinner. Suddenly three or four flowers—cut roses—fell in the midst of us—just as such things sometimes fall in the dark at spiritual seances. But in this case there were several lamps and candles in the room. The ceiling of the hall consisted simply of the solid, bare, painted rafters and boards that supported the flat cement roof of the building. The phenomenon was so wholly unexpected—as unexpected, I am given to understand, by Madame Blavatsky, sitting in an armchair reading at the time, as by the rest of us—that it lost some of the effect it would otherwise have had on our minds. If one could have been told a moment beforehand "now some flowers are going to fall", so that we could have looked up and seen them suddenly appear in the air above our heads, then the impressive effect of an incident so violently out of the common order of things would have been very great. Even as it was, the incident has always remained for those who witnessed it one of the stages on their road to a conviction of the reality of occult powers. Persons to whom it is merely related cannot be expected to rely upon it to any great extent. They will naturally ask various questions as to the construction of the room, who inhabited the house, etc., and even when all these questions had been answered, as they truthfully could be in a manner which would shut out any hypothesis by means of which the fall of the flowers could be explainable by any conjuring trick, there would still be an uncomfortable suspicion left in the questioner's mind as to the completeness of the explanation given. It might hardly have been worth while to bring the incident on to the present record at all, but for the opportunity it affords me of pointing out that the phenomena produced in Madame Blavatsky's presence need not necessarily be of her producing.

Coming now to details in connection with some of the larger mysteries of occultism, I am oppressed by the difficulty of leading up to a statement of what I know now to be facts—as absolute facts as Charing Cross—which shall, nevertheless, be gradual enough not to shock the understanding of people absolutely unused to any but the ordinary grooves of thought as regards physical phenomena. None the less is it true that any "Brother," as the adepts in occultism are familiarly referred to, who may have been seized with the impulse to bestow on our party at Benares the little surprise described above, may have been in Tibet or in the South of India, or anywhere else in the world at the time, and yet just as able to make the roses fall as if he had been in the room with us. I have spoken already of the adept's power of being present "in spirit" as we should say, "in astral body" as an occultist would say, at any distant place in the flash of a moment at will. So present, he can exercise in that distant place some of the psychological powers which he possesses, as completely as he can exercise them in physical body wherever he may actually be, as we understand the expression. I am not pretending to give an explanation of how he produces this or that result, nor for a moment hinting that I know. I am recording merely the certain fact that various occult results have been accomplished in my presence, and explaining as much about them as I have been able to find out. But at all events it has long since become quite plain to me, that wherever Madame Blavatsky is, there the Brothers, wherever they may be, can and constantly do produce phenomena of the most overwhelming sort, with the production of which she herself has little or nothing to do. In reference, indeed, to any phenomenon occurring in her presence, it must be remembered that one can never have any exact knowledge as to how far her own powers may have been employed, or how far she may have been "helped," or whether she has not been quite uninfluential in the production of the result. Precise explanations of this kind are quite contrary to the rules of occultism—which, it must always be remembered, is not trying to convince the world of its existence. In this volume I am trying to convince the world of its existence, but that is another matter altogether. Anyone who wishes to know how the truth really stands can only take up the position of a seeker of truth. He is not a judge before whom occultism comes to plead for credibility. It is useless, therefore, to quarrel with the observations we are enabled to make on the ground that they are not of the kind one would best like to make. The question is whether they yield data on which conclusions may safely rest.

And another consideration claims treatment in connexion with the character of the observations which, so far, I have been enabled to make—that is to say, in connexion with any search for proof of occult power as regards physical phenomena which but for such agency would be miraculous. I can foresee that, in spite of the abject stupidity of the remark, many people will urge that the force of the experiments with which I have had to deal is vitiated because they relate to phenomena which have a certain superficial resemblance to conjuring tricks. Of course this ensues from the fact that conjuring tricks all aim at achieving a certain superficial resemblance to occult phenomena. Let any reader, whatever his present frame of mind on the subject may be, assume for a moment that he has seen reason to conceive that there may be an occult fraternity in existence wielding strange powers over natural forces as yet unknown to ordinary humanity; that this fraternity is bound by rules which cramp the manifestation of these powers, but do not absolutely prohibit it; and then let him propose some comparatively small but scientifically convincing tests which he could ask to have conceded to him as a proof of the reality of some part, at all events, of these powers: it will be found that it is impossible to propose any such test that does not bear a certain superficial resemblance to a conjuring trick. But this will not necessarily impair the value of the test for people capable of dealing with those characteristics of experiments that are not superficial.

The gulf of difference which is really to be observed lying between any of the occult phenomena I shall have to describe presently and a conjuring trick which might imitate it, is due to the fact that the conditions would be utterly unlike. The conjuror would work in his own stage, or in a prepared room. The most remarkable of the phenomena I have had in the presence of Madame Blavatsky have taken place away out of doors in fortuitously chosen places in the woods and on the hills. The conjuror is assisted by any required number of confederates behind his scenes. Madame Blavatsky comes a stranger to Simla, and is a guest in my own house, under my own observation, during the whole of her visit. The conjuror is paid to incur the expenses of accomplishing this or that deception of the senses. Madame Blavatsky is, what I have already explained, a lady of honourable character, instrumental in helping her friends—at their earnest desire wherever phenomena are produced at all—to see some manifestation of the powers in the acquisition of which (instead of earning money by them as the conjuror does with his) she has sacrificed everything the world generally holds dear-station, and so forth, immeasurably above that to which any conjuror or any impostor could aspire. Pursuing Madame Blavatsky with injurious suspicions, persons who resent the occult hypothesis will constantly forget the dictates of common sense in overlooking these considerations.

About the beginning of September 1880, Madame Blavatsky came to Simla as our guest, and in the course of the following six weeks various phenomena occurred, which became the talk of all Anglo-India for a time, and gave rise to some excited feeling on the part of persons who warmly espoused the theory that they must be the result of imposture. It soon became apparent to us that whatever might have been the nature of the restrictions which operated the previous winter at Allahabad to prevent our guest from displaying more than the very least of her powers, these restrictions were now less operative than before. We were soon introduced to a phenomenon we had not been treated to previously. By some modification of the force employed to produce the sound of raps on any object, Madame Blavatsky can produce in the air, without the intermediation of any solid object whatever, the sound of a silvery bell—sometimes a chime or little run of three or four bells on different notes. We had often heard about these bells, but had never heard them produced before. They were produced for us for the first time one evening after dinner while we were still sitting round the table, several times in, succession in the air over our heads, and in one instance instead of the single bell-sound there came one of the chimes of which I speak. Later on I heard them on scores of occasions and in all sorts of different places—in the open air and at different houses where Madame Blavatsky went from time to time. As before with the raps, there is no hypothesis in the case of the bells which can be framed by an adherent of the imposture theory which does not break down on a comparison of the different occasions and conditions under which I have heard them produced. Indeed, the theory of imposture is one which in the matter of the bells has only one narrow conjecture to rest on. Unlike the sound of a rap, which in the ordinary way could be produced by many different methods—so that, to be sure any given example of such a sound is not produced by ordinary means, one has to procure its repetition under a great variety of conditions—the sound of a bell can only be made, physically, in a few ways. You must have a bell, or some sonorous object in the nature of a bell, to make it with. Now, when sitting in a well lighted room, and attentively watching, you get the sound of a bell up above your heads where there is no physical bell to yield it—what are the hypotheses which can attribute the result to trickery. Is the sound really produced outside the room altogether by some agent or apparatus in another. First of all no rational person who had heard this sound would advance that theory, because the sound itself is incompatible with the idea. It is never loud—at least I have never heard it very loud—but it is always clear and distinct to a remarkable extent. If you lightly strike the edge of a thin claret glass with a knife you may get a sound which it would be difficult to persuade anyone had come from another room; but the occult bell-sound is like that, only purer and clearer, with no sub-sound of jarring in it whatever. Independently of this, I have, as I say, heard the sound in the open air produced up in the sky in the stillness of evening. In rooms, it has not always been overhead, but sometimes down on the ground amongst the feet of a group of persons listening for it. Again, on one occasion, when it had been produced two or three times in the drawing-room of a friend's house where we had all been dining, one gentlemen of the party went back to the dining-room two rooms off, to get a finger glass with which to make a sound for the occult bells to repeat—a familiar form of the experiment. While by himself in the dining-room he heard one of the bell-sounds produced near him, though Madame Blavatsky had remained in the drawing-room. This example of the phenomenon satisfactorily disposed of the theory, absurd in itself for persons who frequently heard the bells in all manner of places, that Madame Blavatsky carried some apparatus about her with which to produce the sound. As for the notion of confederacy, that is disposed of by the fact that I have repeatedly heard the sounds when out walking beside Madame Blavatsky's jampan with no other person near us but the jampanees carrying it.

The bell-sounds are not mere sportive illustrations of the properties of the currents which—are set in action to produce them. They serve the direct, practical purpose among occultists of a telegraphic call-bell. It appears that when trained occultists are concerned, so that the mysterious magnetic connection, whatever it may be, which enables them to communicate ideas is once established, they can produce the bell-sounds at any distance in the neighbourhood of the fellow-initiate whose attention they wish to attract. I have repeatedly heard Madame Blavatsky called in this way, when our own little party being alone some evening, we have all been quietly reading. A little "ting" would suddenly sound, and Madame Blavatsky would get up and go to her room to attend to whatever occult business may have been the motive of her summons. A very pretty illustration of the sound, as thus produced by some brother-initiate at a distance, was afforded one evening under these circumstances. A lady, a guest at another house in Simla, had been dining with us, when about eleven o'clock I received a note from her host, enclosing a letter which he asked me to get Madame Blavatsky to send on by occult means to a certain member of the great fraternity to whom both he and I had been writing. I shall explain the circumstances of this correspondence more fully later on. We were all anxious to know at once—before the lady with us that evening returned up the hill, so that she could take back word to her host—whether the letter could be sent; but Madame Blavatsky declared that her own powers would not enable her to perform the feat. The question was whether a certain person, a half-developed brother then in the neighbourhood of Simla, would give the necessary help. Madame Blavatsky said she would see if she could "find him," and taking the letter in her hands, she went out into the veranda, where we all followed her. Leaning on the balustrade, and looking over the wide sweep of the Simla valley, she remained for a few minutes perfectly motionless and silent, as we all were; and the night was far enough advanced for all commonplace sounds to have settled down, so that the stillness was perfect. Suddenly, in the air before us, there sounded the clear note of an occult-bell. "All right," cried Madame, "he will take it." And duly taken the letter was shortly afterwards. But the phenomenon involved in its transmission will be better introduced to the reader in connection with other examples.

I come now to a series of incidents which exhibit occult power in a more striking light than any of those yet described. To a scientific mind, indeed, the production of sounds by means of a force unknown to ordinary science should be as clear a proof that the power in question is a power, as the more sensational phenomena which have to do with the transmission of solid objects by occult agency. The sound can only reach our ears by the vibration of air, and to set up the smallest undulation of air as the effect of a thought will appear to the ordinary understanding as no less outrageous an impossibility than the uprooting of a tree in a similar way. Still there are degrees in wonderfulness which the feelings recognise even if such distinctions are irrational.

The first incident of the kind which I now take up is not one which would in itself be a complete proof of anything for an outsider. I describe it rather for the benefit of readers who may be, either through spiritualistic experiences or in any other way, already alive to the possibility of phenomena as such, and interested rather in experiments which may throw light on their genesis than in mere texts. Managed a little better, the occurrence now to be dealt with would have been a beautiful test; but Madame Blavatsky, left to herself in such matters, is always the worst devisor of tests imaginable. Utterly out of sympathy with the positive and incredulous temperament; engaged all her life in the development amongst Asiatic mystics of the creative rather than the critical faculties, she never can follow the intricate suspicions with which the European observer approaches the consideration of the marvellous in its simplest forms. The marvellous, in forms so stupendously marvellous that they almost elude the grasp of ordinary conceptions, has been the daily food of her life for a great number of years, and it is easy to realise that, for her, the jealous distrust with which ordinary people hunt round the slightest manifestation of occult force to find any loophole through which a suspicion of fraud may creep, as no less tiresome and stupid, then the ordinary person conceives the too credulous spirit to be.

About the end of September my wife went one afternoon with Madame Blavatsky to the top of a neighbouring hill. They were only accompanied by one other friend. I was not present myself on this occasion. While there Madame Blavatsky asked my wife, in a joking way, what was her heart's desire. She said at random and on the spur or the moment, "to get a note from one of the Brothers." Madame Blavatsky took from her pocket a piece of blank pink paper that had been torn off a note received that day. Folding this up into a small compass she took it to the edge of the hill, held it up for a moment or two between her hands and returned saying that it was gone. She presently, after communicating mentally by her own occult methods with the distant Brother, said he asked where my wife would have the letter. At first, she said she should like it to come fluttering down into her lap, but some conversation ensued as to whether this would be the best way to get it, and ultimately it was decided that she should find it in a certain tree. Here, of course, a mistake was made which opens the door to the suspicions of resolutely disbelieving persons. It will be supposed that Madame Blavatsky had some reasons of her own for wishing the tree chosen. For readers who favour that conjecture after all that has gone before, it is only necessary to repeat that the present story is being told not as a proof, but as an incident.

At first, Madame Blavatsky seems to have made a mistake as to the description of the tree, which the distant Brother was indicating as that in which he was going to put the note, and with some trouble my wife scrambled on to the lower branch of a bare and leafless trunk on which nothing could be found. Madame then again got into communication with the Brother and ascertained her mistake. Into another tree at a little distance, which neither Madame nor the one other person present had approached, my wife now climbed a few feet and looked all round among the branches. At first, she saw nothing, but then, turning back her head without moving from the position she had taken up, she saw on a twig immediately before her face—where a moment previously there had been nothing but leaves—a little pink note. This was stuck on to the stalk of a leaf that had been quite freshly torn off, for the stalk was still green and moist—not withered as it would have been if the leaf had been torn off for any length of time. The note was found to contain these few words: "I have been asked to leave a note here for you. What can I do for you?", It was signed by some Tibetan characters. The pink paper on which it was written appeared to be the same which Madame Blavatsky had taken blank from her pocket shortly before.

How was it transmitted first to the Brother who wrote upon it and then back again to the top of our hill? not to speak of the mystery of its attachment to the tree in the way described. So far as I can frame conjectures on this subject, it would be premature to set them forth in detail till I have gone more fully into the facts observed. It is no use to discuss the way the wings of flying-fish are made for people who will not believe in the reality of flying fish at all, and refuse to accept phenomena less guaranteed by orthodoxy than Pharaoh's chariot wheels.

I come now to the incidents of a very remarkable day. The day before, I should explain, we started on a little expedition which turned out a *coup manqué*, though, but for some tiresome mishaps, it might have led, we afterwards had reason to think, to some very interesting results. We mistook our way to a place of which Madame Blavatsky had received an imperfect description—or a description she imperfectly understood—in an occult conversation with one of the Brothers then actually passing through Simla. Had we gone the right way that day we might have had the good fortune of meeting him, for he stayed one night at a certain old Tibetan temple, or rest-house, such as is often found about the Himalayas, and which the blind apathy of commonplace English people leads them to regard as of no particular interest or importance. Madame Blavatsky was wholly unacquainted with Simla, and the account she gave us of the place she wanted to go to led us to think she meant a different place. We started, and for a long time Madame declared that we must be going in the right direction because she felt certain currents. Afterwards it appeared that the road to the place we were making for, and to that for which we ought to have made, were coincident for a considerable distance; but a slight divergence at one point carried us into a wholly wrong system of hill-paths. Eventually Madame utterly lost her scent: we tried back; we who knew Simla discussed its topography and wondered where it could be she wanted to get to, but all to no purpose. We launched ourselves down a hillside where Madame declared she once more felt the missing current; but occult currents may flow where travellers cannot pass, and when we attempted this descent. I knew the case was desperate. After a while the expedition had to be abandoned, and we went home much disappointed.

Why, some one may ask, could not the omniscient Brother feel that Madame was going wrong, and direct us properly in time? I say this question will be asked, because I know from experience that people unused to the subject will not bear in mind the relations of the Brothers to such inquirers as ourselves. In this case, for example, the situation was not *one* in which the Brother in question was anxiously waiting to prove his existence to a jury of intelligent Englishmen. We can learn so little about the daily life of an adept in occultism, that we who are uninitiated can tell very little about the interests that really engage his attention; but we can find out this much—that his attention is constantly engaged on interests connected with his own work, and the gratification of the curiosity concerning occult matters of persons who are not regular students of occultism forms no part of that work at all. On the contrary, unless under very exceptional conditions, he is even forbidden to make any concessions whatever to such curiosity. In the case in point the course of events may probably have been something of this kind:—Madame Blavatsky perceived by her own occult tentacle that one of her illustrious friends was in the neighbourhood. She immediately—having a sincere desire to oblige us—may have asked him whether she might bring us to see him. Probably he would regard any such request very much as the astronomer royal might regard the request of a friend to bring a party of ladies to look through his telescopes; but nonetheless he might say, to please his half-fledged "brother" in occultism, Madame Blavatsky, "Very well, bring them, if you like: I am in such and such a place." And then he would go on with his work, remembering afterwards that the intended visit had never been paid, and perhaps turning an occult perception in the direction of the circumstances to ascertain what had happened.

However, this may have been, the expedition as first planned broke down. It was not with the hope of seeing the Brother, but on the general principle of hoping for something to turn up, that we arranged to go for a picnic the following day in another direction, which, as the first road had failed, we concluded to be probably the one we ought to have taken previously.

We set out at the appointed time next morning. We were originally to have been a party of six, but a seventh person joined us just before we started. After going down the hill for some hours a place was chosen in the wood near the upper waterfall for our breakfast: the baskets that had been brought with us were unpacked, and, as usual at an Indian picnic, the servants at a little distance lighted a fire and set to work to make tea and coffee. Concerning this some joking arose over the fact that we had one cup and saucer too few, on account of the seventh person who joined us at starting, and some one laughingly asked Madame Blavatsky to create another cup and saucer. There was no set purpose in the proposal at first, but when Madame Blavatsky said it would be very difficult, but that if we liked she would try, attention was of course at once arrested. Madame Blavatsky, as usual, held mental conversation with one of the Brothers, and then wandered a little about in the immediate neighbourhood of where we were sitting—that is to say, within a radius of half-a-dozen to a dozen yards from our picnic cloth—I'm closely following, waiting to see what would happen. Then she marked a spot on the ground, and called to one of the gentlemen of the party to bring a knife to dig with. The place chosen was the edge of a little slope covered with thick weeds and grass and shrubby undergrowth. The gentleman with the knife—let us call him X-------------- as I shall have to refer to him afterwards—tore up these in the first place with some difficulty, as the roots were tough and closely interlaced. Cutting then into the matted roots and earth with the knife, and pulling away the *débris* with his hands, he came at last, on the edge of something white, which turned out, as it was completely excavated, to be the required cup. A corresponding saucer was also found after a little more digging. Both objects were in among the roots which spread everywhere through the ground, so that it seemed as if the roots were growing round them. The cup and saucer both corresponded exactly, as regards their pattern, with those that had been brought to the picnic, and constituted a seventh cup and saucer when brought back to where we were to have breakfast. I may as well add at once that afterwards, when we got home, my wife questioned our principal khitmutgar as to how many cups and saucers of that particular kind we possessed. In the progress of years, as the set was an old set, some had been broken, but the man at once said that nine teacups were left. When collected and counted that number was found to be right, without reckoning the excavated cup. That made ten, and as regards the pattern—it was one of a somewhat peculiar kind, bought a good many years previously in London, and which assuredly could never have been matched in Simla.

Now, the notion that human beings can create material objects by the exercise of mere psychological power, will of course be revolting to the understandings of people to whom this whole subject is altogether strange. It is not making the idea much more acceptable to say that the cup and saucer appear in this case to have been "doubled" rather than created. The doubling of objects seems merely another kind of creation—creation according to a pattern. However, the facts, the occurrences of the morning I have described, were at all events exactly as I have related them. I have been careful as to the strict and minute truthfulness of every detail. If the phenomenon was not what it appeared to be—a most wonderful display of a power of which the modern scientific world has no comprehension whatever it was, of course, an elaborate fraud. That supposition, however, setting aside the moral impossibility from any point of view of assuming Madame Blavatsky capable of participation in such an imposture, will only bear to be talked of vaguely. As a way out of the dilemma it will not serve any person of ordinary intelligence who is aware of the facts, or who trusts my statement of them. The cup and saucer were assuredly dug up in the way I describe. If they were not deposited there by occult agency, they must have been buried there beforehand. Now, I have described the character of the ground from which they were dug up; assuredly that had been undisturbed for years by the character of the vegetation upon it. But it may be urged that from some other part of the sloping ground a sort of tunnel may have been excavated in the first instance through which the cup and saucer could have been thrust into the place where they were found. Now this theory is barely tenable as regards its physical possibility. If the tunnel had been big enough for the purpose it would have left traces which were not perceptible on the ground—which were not even discoverable when the ground was searched shortly afterwards with a view to that hypothesis. But the truth is that the theory of previous burial is morally untenable in view of the fact that the demand for the cup and saucer—of all the myriad things that might have been asked for—could never have been foreseen. It arose out of circumstances themselves the sport of the moment. If no extra person had joined us at the last moment the number of cups and saucers packed up by the servants would have been sufficient for our needs, and no attention would have been drawn to them. It was by the servants, without the knowledge of any guest, that the cups taken were chosen from others that might just as easily have been taken. Had the burial fraud been really perpetrated it would have been necessary to constrain us to choose the *exact* spot we did actually choose for the picnic with a view to the previous preparations, but the exact spot on which the ladies' jampans were deposited was chosen by myself in concert with the gentleman referred to above as X—, and it was within a few yards of this spot that the cup was found. Thus, leaving the other absurdities of the fraud hypothesis out of sight, who could be the agents employed to deposit the cup and saucer in the ground, and when did they perform the operation? Madame Blavatsky was under our roof the whole time from the previous evening when the picnic was determined on to the moment of starting. The one personal servant she had with her, a Bombay boy and a perfect stranger to Simla, was constantly about the house the previous evening, and from the first awakening of the household in the morning—and as it happened he spoke to my own bearer in the middle of the night, for I had been annoyed by a loft door which had been left unfastened, and was slamming in the wind, and called up servants to shut it. Madame Blavatsky it appears, thus awakened, had sent her servant, who always slept within call, to inquire what was the matter. Colonel Olcott, the President of the Theosophical Society, also a guest of ours at the time of which I am speaking, was certainly with us all the evening from the period of our return from the abortive expedition of the afternoon, and was also present at the start. To imagine that he spent the night in going four or five miles down a difficult *khud* through forest paths difficult to find, to bury a cup and saucer of a kind that we were not likely to take in a place we were not likely to go to, in order that in the exceedingly remote contingency of its being required for the perpetration of a hoax it might be there, would certainly be a somewhat extravagant conjecture. Another consideration—the destination for which we were making can be approached by two roads from opposite ends of the upper horseshoe of hills on which Simla stands. It was open to us to select either path, and certainly neither Madame Blavatsky nor Colonel Olcott had any share in the selection of that actually taken. Had we taken the other, we should never have come to the spot where we actually picnicked.

The hypothesis of fraud in this affair is, as I have said, a defiance of common sense when worked out in any imaginable way. The extravagance of this explanation will, moreover, be seen to heighten as my narrative proceeds, and as the incident just related is compared with others which took place later. But I have not yet done with the incidents of the cup-morning.

The gentleman called X ----------------------------had been a good deal with us during the week or two that had already elapsed since Madame Blavatsky's arrival. Like many of our friends, he had been greatly impressed with much he had seen in her presence. He had especially come to the conclusion that the Theosophical Society, in which she was interested, was exerting a good influence with the natives, a view which he had expressed more than once in warm language in my presence. He had declared his intention of joining this Society as I had done myself. Now, when the cup and saucer were found most of us who were present, X among the number, were greatly impressed, and in the conversation that ensued the idea arose that X—might formally become a member of the Society then and there. I should not have taken part in this suggestion—I believe I originated it—if X ---------- had not in cool blood decided, as I understood, to join the Society; in itself, moreover, a step which involved no responsibilities whatever, and simply indicated sympathy with the pursuit of occult knowledge and a general adhesion to broadly philanthropic doctrines of brotherly sentiments towards all humanity, irrespective of race and creed. This has to be explained in view of some little annoyances which followed.

The proposal that X ------------should then and there formally join the Society was one with which he was quite ready to fall in. But some documents were required-a formal diploma, the gift of which to a new member should follow his initiation into certain little Masonic forms of recognition adopted in the Society.

How could we get a diploma? Of course for the group then present a difficulty of this sort was merely another opportunity for the exercise of Madame's powers. Could she get a diploma brought to us by "magic?" After an occult conversation with the Brother who had then interested himself in our proceedings,Madame told us that the diploma would be forthcoming. She described the appearance it would present—a roll of paper wound round with an immense quantity of string, and then bound up in the leaves of a creeping plant. We should find it about in the woods where we were, and we could all look for it, but it would be X—, for whom it was intended, who would find it. Thus it fell out. We all searched about in the undergrowth or in the trees, wherever fancy prompted us to look, and it was X—who found the roll, done up as described.

We had had our breakfast by this time. X— was formally "initiated" a member of the society by Colonel Olcott, and after a time we shifted our quarters to a lower place in the wood where there was the little Tibetan temple, or rest-house, which the Brother who had been passing through Simla—according to what Madame Blavatsky told us—had passed the previous night. We amused ourselves by examining—the little building inside and out, "bathing in the "good magnetism," as Madame Blavatsky expressed it, and then, lying on the grass outside, it occurred to someone that we wanted more coffee. The servants were told to prepare some, but it appeared that they had used up all our water. The water to be found in the streams near Simla is not of a kind to be used for purposes of this sort, and for a picnic, clean filtered water is always taken out in bottles, It appears that all the bottles in our baskets had been exhausted. This report was promptly verified by the servants by the exhibition of the empty bottles. The only thing to be done was to send to a brewery, the nearest building, about a mile off, and ask for water. I wrote a pencil note and a coolie went off with the empty bottles. Time passed, and the coolie returned, to our great disgust, without the water. There had been no European left at the brewery that day (It was Sunday) to receive the note, and the coolie had stupidly plodded back with the empty bottles under his arm, instead of asking about and finding someone able to supply the required water.

At this time our party was a little dispersed. X— and one of the other gentlemen had wandered off. No one of the remainder of the party was expecting fresh phenomena, when Madame suddenly got up, went over to the baskets, a dozen or twenty yards off, picked out a bottle-one of those, I believe, which had been brought back by the coolie empty—and came back to us holding it under the fold of her dress. Laughingly producing it, it was found to be full of water. Just like a conjuring trick, will some one say? Just like, except for the conditions. For such a conjuring trick, the conjurer defines the thing to be done. In our ease the want of water was as unforeseeable in the first instance as the want of the cup and saucer. The accident that left the brewery deserted by its Europeans, and the further accident that the coolie sent up for water should have been so abnormally stupid even for a coolie as to come back without, because there happened to be no European to take my note, were accidents but for which the opportunity for obtaining the water by occult agency could not have arisen. And those accidents supervened on the fundamental accident, improbable in itself, that our servants should have sent us out insufficiently supplied. That any bottle of water could have been left unnoticed at the bottom of the baskets is a suggestion that I can hardly imagine anyone present putting forward, for the servants had been found fault with for not bringing enough; they had just before had the baskets completely emptied out, and we had not submitted to the situation till we had been fully satisfied that there really was no more water left. Furthermore, I tasted the water in the bottle Madame Blavatsky produced, and it was not water of the same kind as that which came from our own filters. It was an earthy tasting water, unlike that of the modern Simla supply, but equally unlike, I may add, though in a different way, the offensive and discoloured water of the only stream flowing through those woods.

How was it brought? The how, of course, in all these cases is the great mystery which I am unable to explain except in general terms; but the impossibility of understanding the way adepts manipulate matter is one thing; the impossibility of denying that they do manipulate it in a manner which Western ignorance would describe as miraculous is another. The fact is there whether we can explain it or not. The rough, popular saying that you cannot argue the hind leg off a cow, embodies a sound reflection, which our prudent sceptics in matters of the kind with which I am now dealing are too apt to overlook. You cannot argue away a fact by contending that by the lights in your mind it ought to be something different from what it is. Still less can you argue away a mass of facts like those I am now recording by a series of extravagant and contradictory hypotheses about each in turn. What the determined disbeliever so often overlooks is that the scepticism which may show an acuteness of mind up to a certain point, reveals a deficient intelligence when adhered to in face of certain kinds of evidence.

I remember when the phonograph was first invented, a scientific officer in the service of the Indian Government sent me an article he had written on the earliest accounts received of the instrument—to prove that the story must be a hoax, because the instrument described was scientifically impossible. He had worked out the times of vibrations required to reproduce the sounds and so on, and very intelligently argued that the alleged result was unattainable. But when phonographs in due time were imported into India, he did not continue to say they were impossible, and that there must be a man shut up in each machine, even though there did not seem to be room. That last is the attitude of the self-complacent people who get over the difficulty about the causation of occult and spiritual phenomena by denying, in face of the palpable experience of thousands—in face of the testimony in shelves—full of books that they do not read—that any such phenomena take place at all.

X—, I should add here, afterwards changed his mind about the satisfactory character of the cup phenomena, and said he thought it vitiated as a scientific proof by the interposition of the theory that the cup and saucer might have been thrust up into their places by means of a tunnel cut from a lower part of the bank. I have discussed that hypothesis already, and mention the fact of X—'s change of opinion, which does not affect any of the circumstances I have narrated, merely to avoid the chance that readers, who may have heard or read about the Simla phenomenon in other pages, might think I was treating the change of opinion in question as something which it was worth while to disguise. And, indeed, the convictions which I ultimately attained were themselves the result of accumulated experiences I have yet to relate, so that I cannot tell how far my own certainty concerning the reality of occult power rests on anyone example that I have seen.

It was on the evening of the day of the cup phenomenon that there occurred an incident destined to become the subject of very wide discussion in all the Anglo-Indian papers. This was the celebrated "brooch incident." The facts were related at the time in a little statement drawn up for publication, and signed by the nine persons who witnessed it! This statement will be laid before the reader directly, but as the comments to which it gave rise showed that it was too meagre to convey a full and accurate idea of what occurred, I will describe the course of events a little more fully. In doing this, I may use names with a certain freedom, as these were all appended to the published document.

We, that is, my wife and myself with our guest, had gone up the hill to dine, in accordance with previous engagements, with Mr. and Mrs. Hume. We dined, a party of eleven, at a round table, and Madame Blavatsky, sitting next our host, tired and out of spirits as it happened, was unusually silent. During the beginning of dinner she scarcely said a word, Mr. Hume conversing chiefly with the lady on his other hand. It is a common trick at Indian dinner-tables to have little metal plate warmers with hot water before each guest, on which each plate served remains while in use. Such plate warmers were used on the evening I am describing, and over hers—in an interval during which plates had been removed—Madame Blavatsky was absently warming her hands. Now, the production of Madame Blavatsky's raps and bell-sounds we had noticed sometimes seemed easier and the effects better when her hands had been warmed in this way; so some one, seeing her engaged in warming them, asked her some question, hinting in an indirect way at phenomena. I was very far from expecting anything of the kind that evening, and Madame Blavatsky was equally far from intending to do anything herself or from expecting any display at the hands of one of the Brothers. So, merely in mockery, when asked why she was warming her hands, she enjoined us all to warm our hands too and see what would happen. Some of the people present actually did so, a few joking words passing among them. Then Mrs. Hume raised a little laugh by holding up her hands and saying, "But I have warmed my hands, what next". Now Madame Blavatsky, as I have said, was not in a mood for any occult performances at all, but it appears from what I learned afterwards that just at this moment, or immediately before, she suddenly perceived by those occult faculties of which mankind at large have no knowledge, that one of the Brothers was present "in astral body" invisible to the rest of us in the room. It was following his indications, therefore, that she acted in what followed; of course no one knew at the time that she had received any impulse in the matter external to herself. What took place as regards the surface of things was simply this: When Mrs. Hume said what I have set down above, and when the little laugh ensued, Madame Blavatsky put out her hand across the one person sitting between herself and Mrs. Hume and took one of that lady's hands, saying, "Well then, do you wish for anything in particular? or as the lawyers say," words to that effect." I cannot repeat the precise sentences spoken, nor can I say now exactly what Mrs. Hume first replied before she quite understood the situation; but this was made clear in a very few minutes. Some of the other people present catching this first, explained, "Think of something you would like to have brought to you; anything you like not wanted for any mere worldly motive; is there anything you can think of that will be very difficult to get?" Remarks of this sort were the only kind that were made in the short interval that elapsed between the remark by Mrs. Hume about having warmed her hands and the indication by her of the thing she had thought of. She said then that she had thought of something that would do. What was it? An old brooch that her mother had given her long ago and that she had lost.

Now, when this brooch, which was ultimately recovered by occult agency, as the rest of my story will show, came to be talked about, people said:— "Of course Madame Blavatsky led up the conversation to the particular thing she had arranged before-hand to produce." I have described *all* the conversation which took place on this subject, before the brooch was named. There was no conversation about the brooch or any other thing of the kind whatever. Five minutes before the brooch was named, there had been no idea in the mind of any person present that any phenomenon in the nature of finding any lost article, or of any other kind, indeed, was going to be performed. Nor while Mrs. Hume was going over in her mind the things she might ask for, did she speak any word indicating the direction her thoughts were taking.

From the point of the story now reached the narrative published at the time tells it almost as fully as it need be told, and, at all events, with a simplicity that will assist the reader in grasping all the facts—so I reprint it here in full—

> "On Sunday, the 3rd of October, at Mr. Hume's house at Simla, there were present at dinner Mr. and Mrs. Hume, Mr. and Mrs. Sinnett, Mrs. Gordon, Mr. F. Hogg, Captain P.J. Maitland, Mr. Beatson, Mr. Davidson, Colonel Olcott, and Madame Blavatsky. Most of the persons present having recently seen many remarkable occurrences In Madame Blavatsky's presence, conversation turned on occult phenomena, and in the course of this Madame Blavatsky asked Mrs. Hume if there was anything she particularly wished for. Mrs. Hume at first hesitated, but in a short time said there was something she would particularly like to have brought her, namely, a small article of jewellery that she formerly possessed, but had given away to a person who had allowed it to pass out of her possession. Madame Blavatsky then said if she would fix the image of the article in question very definitely on her mind, she, Madame Blavatsky, would endeavour to procure It. Mrs. Hume then said that she vividly remembered the article, and described it as an old-fashioned breast brooch set round with pearls, With glass at the front, and the back made to contain hair. She then, on being asked, drew a rough sketch of the brooch.
>
> Madame Blavatsky then wrapped up a coin attached to her watch-chain In two cigarette papers, and put it in her dress, and said that she hoped the brooch might be obtained in the course of the evening. At the close of dinner she said to Mr. Hume that the paper in which the corn had been wrapped was gone. A little later, in the drawing room, she said that the brooch would not be brought into the house, but that it must be looked for in the garden, and then as the party went out accompanying her, she said she had clairvoyantly seen the brooch fall

into a star-shaped bed of flowers. Mr. Hume led the way to such a bed in a distant part of the garden. A prolonged and careful search was made with lanterns, and eventually a small paper packet, consisting of two cigarette papers, was found amongst the leaves by Mrs. Sinnett. This being opened on the spot was found to contain a brooch exactly corresponding to the previous description, and which Mrs. Hume Identified as that which she had originally lost. None of the party, except Mr. and Mrs. Hume, had ever seen or heard of the brooch. Mr. Hume had not thought of it for years. Mrs. Hume had never spoken of it to anyone since she parted with it, nor had she, for long, even thought of it. She herself stated, after it was found, that it was only when Madame asked her whether there was anything she would like to have, that the remembrance of this brooch, the gift of her mother, flashed across her mind.

"Mrs. Hume is not a spiritualist, and up to the time of the occurrence described was no believer either in occult phenomena or in Madame Blavatsky's powers. The conviction of all present was, that the occurrence was of an absolutely unimpeachable character, as an evidence of the truth of the possibility of occult phenomena. The brooch is unquestionably the one which Mrs, Hume lost. Even supposing, which is practically impossible, that the article, lost months before Mrs. Hume ever heard of Madame Blavatsky, and bearing no letters or other indication of original ownership, could have passed in a natural way into Madame Blavatsky's possession, even then she could not possibly have foreseen that it would be asked for, and Mrs. Hume herself had not given it a thought for months

"This narrative, read over to the party, is signed by—

A. O. HUME,
ALICE GORDON,
M. A. HUME,
P. J.:MAITLAND, FRED. R. HOGG, WM. DAVIDSON,
A. P. SINNETT, STUART BEATSON. PATIENCE SINNETT.

It is needless to state that when this narrative was published the nine persons above mentioned were assailed with torrents of ridicule, the effect of which, however; has not been in any single case to modify, in the smallest degree, the conviction which their signatures attested at the time, that the incident related was a perfectly conclusive proof of the reality of occult power. Floods of more or less imbecile criticism have been directed to show that the whole performance must have been a trick; and for many persons in India it is now, no doubt, an established explanation that Mrs. Hume was adroitly led up to ask for the particular article produced, by a quantity of preliminary talk about a feat which Madame Blavatsky specially went to the house to perform. A further established opinion with a certain section of the Indian public is, that the brooch which it appears Mrs. Hume gave to her daughter, and which her daughter lost, must have been got from that young lady about a year previously, when she passed through Bombay, where Madame Blavatsky was living, on her way to England. The young lady's testimony to the effect that she lost the brooch before she went to Bombay, or ever saw Madame Blavatsky, is a little feature of this hypothesis which its contented framers do not care to enquire into. Nor do persons who think the fact that the brooch once belonged to Mrs. Hume's daughter, and that this young lady once saw Madame Blavatsky at Bombay, sufficiently "suspicious" to wipe out the effect of the whole incident as described above-ever attempt, as far as I have discerned, to trace out a coherent chain of events as illuminated by their suspicions, or to compare these with the circumstances of the brooch's actual recovery. No care, however, to arrange the circumstances of an occult demonstration so that the possibility of fraud and delusion may really be excluded, is sufficient to exclude the imputation of this afterwards by people for whom any argument, however illogical really, is good enough to attack a strange idea with.

As regards the witnesses of the brooch phenomenon the conditions were so perfect that when they were speculating as to the objections which might be raised by the public when the story should come to be told, they did not foresee either of the objections actually raised afterwards—the leading up in conversation theory, and the theory about Miss Hume having—put Madame Blavatsky in possession of the brooch. They knew that there had been no previous conversation at all about the brooch or any other proposed feat, that the idea about getting something Mrs. Hume should ask for, arose all in a moment, and that almost immediately afterwards, the brooch was named. As for Miss Hume having unconsciously contributed to the production of the phenomenon, it did not occur to the witnesses that this would be suggested, because they did not foresee that anyone could be so foolish as to shut their eyes to the important circumstances, to concentrate their attention entirely on one of quite minor importance. As the statement itself says, even supposing, which is practically impossible, that the brooch could have passed into Madame Blavatsky's possession in a natural way, she could not possibly have foreseen that it would have been asked for.

The only conjectures the witnesses could frame to explain beforehand the tolerably certain result that the public at large would refuse to be convinced by the brooch incident, were that they might be regarded as misstating the facts and omitting some which the superior intelligence of their critics—as their critics would regard the matter—would see to upset the significance of the rest, or that Mrs. Hume must be a confederate. Now, this last conjecture, which will no doubt occur to readers in England, had only to be stated, to be, for the other persons concerned in the incident, one of the most amusing results to which it could give rise. We all knew Mrs. Hume to be as little predisposed towards any such a conspiracy as she was morally incapable of the wrongdoing it would involve.

At one stage of the proceedings, moreover, we had considered the question as to the extent to which the conditions of the phenomenon were satisfactory. It had often happened that faults had eventually been found with Madame Blavatsky's phenomena by reason of some oversight in the conditions that had not been thought of at first. One of our friends, therefore, on the occasion I am describing, had suggested, after we rose from the dinner-table, that before going any further the company generally should be asked whether, if the brooch could be produced, that would under the circumstances be a satisfactory proof of occult agency in the matter. We carefully reviewed the matter in which the situation had been developed and we all came to the conclusion that the test, would be absolutely complete, and that on this occasion there was no weak place in the chain of the argument. Then it was that Madame Blavatsky said the brooch would be brought to the garden, and that we could go out and search for it.

An interesting circumstance for those who had already watched some of the other phenomena I have described was this: The brooch, as stated above, was found wrapped up in two cigarette papers, and these, when examined in a full light in the house, were found still to bear the mark of the coin attached to Madame Blavatsky's watch chain, which had been wrapped up in them before they departed on their mysterious errand. They were thus identified for people who had got over the first stupendous difficulty of believing in the possibility of transporting material objects by occult agency as the same papers that had been seen by us at the dinner-table.

The occult transmission of objects to a distance not being, "magic", as Western readers understand the word, is susceptible of some partial explanation even for ordinary readers, for whom the means by which the forces employed are manipulated must remain entirely mysterious. It is not contended that the currents which are made use of, convey the bodies transmitted in a solid mass just as they exist for the senses. The body, to be transmitted, is supposed first to be disintegrated, conveyed on the currents in infinitely minute particles, and then reintegrated at its destination. In the case of the brooch, the first thing to be done must have been to find it. This, however, would simply be a feat of clairvoyance—the scent of the object, so to speak, being taken up from the person who spoke of it and had once possessed it—and there is no clairvoyance of which the western world has any knowledge, comparable in its vivid intensity to the clairvoyance of an adept in occultism. Its resting-place thus discovered, the disintegration process would come into play, and the object desired would be conveyed to the place where the adept engaged with it would choose to have it deposited. The part played in the phenomenon by the cigarette papers would be this: In order that we might be able to find the brooch, it was necessary to connect it by an occult scent with Madame Blavatsky. The cigarette papers, which she always carried about with her, were thus impregnated with her magnetism, and taken from her by the Brother, left an occult trail behind them. Wrapped round the brooch, they conducted this trail to the required spot.

The magnetisation of the cigarette papers always with her, enabled Madame Blavatsky to perform a little feat with them which was found by everyone for whom it was done an exceedingly complete bit of evidence; though here again the superficial resemblance of the experiment to a conjuring trick misled the intelligence of ordinary persons who read about the incidents referred to in the newspapers. The feat itself may be most conveniently discussed by the quotation of three letters, which appeared in the *Pioneer* of the 23rd of October, and were as follows;—

"S<small>IR</small>,

> —The account of the discovery of Mrs. Hume's brooch has called forth several letters, and many questions have been asked, some of which I may answer on a future occasion, but I think it only right to first contribute further testimony to the occult powers possessed by Madame Blavatsky. In thus coming before the public, one must be prepared for ridicule, but it is a weapon which we who know something of these matters can well afford to despise. On Thursday last, at about half-past ten o'clock, I was sitting in Madame Blavatsky's room conversing with her, and in a casual way asked her if she would

be able to send me anything by occult means when I returned to my home. She said "No", and explained to me some of the laws under which she acts, one being that she must know the place and have been there—the more recently the better—in order to establish a magnetic current: She then recollected that she had been somewhere that morning, and after a moment's reflection remembered whose house it was she had visited.[1] She said she could send a cigarette there, if I would go *at once* to verify the fact. I of course, consented. I must here mention that I had seen her do this kind of thing once before; and the reason she gives for sending *cigarettes* is, that the paper and tobacco being always about her person, are highly magnetised, and therefore more amenable to her power, which she most emphatically declares is not super-natural, but merely the manifestation of laws unknown to us. To continue my story. She took out a cigarette paper and slowly tore oft a corner as zigzag as possible, I never taking my eyes off her hands. She gave me the corner, which I at once put into an envelope, and it never left my possession I can declare. She made the cigarette with the remainder of the paper, She then said she would try an experiment which might not succeed, but the failure would be of no consequence with me. She then most certainly put that cigarette into the fire, and I saw it burn, and I started at once to the gentleman's house, scarcely able to believe that I should find in the place indicated by her the counterpart of the cigarette paper I had with me; but sure enough there it was, and, in the presence of the gentleman and his wife, I opened out the cigarette and found my corner piece fitted exactly. It would be useless to try and explain any theory in connection with these phenomena, and it would be unreasonable to expect anyone to believe in them, unless their own experience had proved the possibility of such wonders. All one asks or expects is, that a few of the more intelligent members of the community may be led to look into the vast amount of evidence now accumulated of the phenomena taking place all over Europe and America. It seems a pity that the majority should be in such utter ignorance of these facts; it is within the power of anyone visiting England to convince himself of their truth.

ALICE GORDON

"SIR,

—I have been asked to give an account of a circumstance which took place in my presence on the 13th instant. On the evening of that day I was sitting alone with Madame Blavatsky and Colonel Olcott in the drawing-room of Mr. Sinnett's house in Simla. After some conversation on various matters, Madame Blavatsky said she would like to try an experiment in a manner which had been suggested to her by Mr. Sinnett. She, therefore, took two cigarette papers from her pocket and marked on each of them a number of parallel lines in pencil. She then tore a piece off the end of each paper across the lines, and gave them to me. At that time Madame Blavatsky was sitting close to me, and I intently watched her proceedings, my eyes being not more than two feet from her hands. She declined to let me mark or tear the papers alleging that if handled by others they would become imbued with their personal magnetism, which would counterset her own. However, the torn pieces were handed directly to me, and I could not observe any opportunity for the substitution of other papers by sleight of hand. The genuineness or otherwise of the phenomena afterwards presented appears to rest on this point. The torn off pieces of the paper remained in my closed left hand until the conclusion of the experiment. Of the larger pieces Madame Blavatsky made two cigarettes, giving the first to me to hold while the other was being made up. I scrutinised this cigarette very attentively, in order to be able to recognise it afterwards. The cigarettes being finished, Madame Blavatsky stood up, and took them between her hands, which she rubbed together. After about twenty or thirty seconds, the grating noise of the paper, at first distinctly audible, ceased. She then said the current[2] is passing round this end of the room, and I can only send them somewhere near here. A moment afterwards she said one had fallen on the piano, the other near that bracket. As I sat on a sofa with my back to the wall, the piano was opposite, and the bracket, supporting a few pieces of china, was to the right, between it and the door. Both were in full view across the rather narrow room. The top of the piano was covered with piles of music books, and it was among these Madame Blavatsky thought a cigarette would be found; The books were removed, one by one, by myself, but without seeing anything. I then opened the piano, and found a cigarette on a narrow shelf inside it. This cigarette I took out and recognised as the one I had held in my hand. The other was found in a covered cup on the bracket. Both cigarettes were still damp where—they had been moistened at the edges in the process of manufacture. I took the cigarettes to a table, without permitting them to be touched or even seen by Madame Blavatsky and Colonel Olcott. On being unrolled and smoothed out, the torn, jagged edges were found to fit exactly to the pieces that I had all this time retained in my hand. The pencil marks also corresponded. It would therefore appear that the papers were actually the same as those I had seen torn. Both the papers are still in my possession. It may be added that Colonel Olcott sat near me with his back to Madame Blavatsky during the experiment, and did not move till it was concluded.

"P. J. MAITLAND, *Captain*."

"SIR,

—With reference to the correspondence now filling your columns, on the subject of Madame Blavatsky's recent manifestations, it may interest your readers if I record a striking incident which took place last week in my presence. I had occasion to call on Madame, and in the course of our interview she tore off a corner from a cigarette paper, asking me to hold the same, which I did. With the remainder of the paper she prepared a cigarette in the ordinary manner, and in a few moments caused this cigarette to disappear from her hands. We were sitting at the time in the drawing-room. I inquired if it were likely to find this cigarette again, and after a short pause Madame requested me to accompany her into the dining-room, where the cigarette would be found on the top of a curtain hanging over the window. By means of a table and a chair placed thereon, I was enabled with some difficulty to reach and take down a cigarette from the place indicated. This cigarette I opened, and found the paper to correspond exactly with that I had seen a few minutes before in the drawing-room. That is to say, the corner-piece, which I had retained in my possession, fitted exactly into the jagged edges of the torn paper in which the tobacco had been rolled. To the best of my belief, the test was as complete and satisfactory as any test can be. I refrain from giving my opinion as to the causes which produced the effect, feeling sure that your readers who take an interest in these phenomena will prefer exercising their own judgement in the matter. I merely give you an unvarnished statement of what I saw. I may be permitted to add I am not a member of the Theosophist Society, nor, so far as I know, am I biassed in favour of occult science, although a warm sympathiser with the proclaimed objects of the Society over which Colonel Olcott presides.

"CHARLES FRANCIS MASSY."

Of course, anyone familiar with conjuring will be aware that an imitation of this "trick" can be arranged by a person gifted with a little sleight of hand. You take two pieces of paper, and tear off a corner of both together, so that the jags of both are the same. You make a cigarette with one piece, and put it in the place where you mean to have it ultimately found. You then hold the other piece underneath the one you tear in presence of the spectator, slip in one of the already torn corners into his hand instead of that he sees you tear, make your cigarette with the other part of the original piece, dispose of that anyhow you please, and allow the prepared cigarette to be found. Other variations of the system may be readily imagined, and for persons who have not actually seen Madame Blavatsky do one of her cigarette feats it may be useless to point out that she does not do them as a conjuror would, and that the spectator, if he is gifted with ordinary common sense, can never have the faintest shadow of a doubt about the corner given to him being the corner torn off—a certainty which the pencil—marks upon it, drawn before his eyes, would enhance, if that were necessary. However, as I say, though experience shows me that the outsider is prone to regard the little cigarette phenomenon as "suspicious," it has never failed to be regarded as convincing by the most acute people among those who have witnessed it. With all phenomena, however, stupidity on the part of the observer will defeat any attempt to reach his understanding, no matter how perfect the tests supplied.

I realise this more fully now than at the time of which I am writing. Then I was chiefly anxious to get experiments arranged, which should be really complete in their details and leave no opening for the suggestion even of imposture. It was "an uphill struggle first, because Madame Blavatsky was intractable and excitable as an experimentalist, and herself no more than the recipient of favours from the Brothers in reference to the greater phenomena. And it seemed to me conceivable that the Brothers might themselves not always realise precisely the frame of mind in which persons of European training approached the consideration of such miracles as these with which we were dealing, so that they did not always make sufficient allowance for the necessity of rendering their test phenomena quite perfect and unassailable in all minor details. I knew, of course, that they were not primarily anxious to convince the commonplace world of anything whatever; but still they frequently did assist Madame Blavatsky to produce phenomena that had no other motive except the production of an effect on the minds of people belonging to the outer world; and it seemed to me that under these circumstances they might just as well do something that would leave no room for the imputation even of any trickery.

One day, therefore, I asked Madame Blavatsky whether if I wrote a letter to one of the Brothers explaining my views, she could get it delivered for me. I hardly thought this was probable, as I knew how very unapproachable the Brothers generally are; but as she said that at any rate she would try, I wrote a letter, addressing it "to the Unknown Brother," and gave it to her to see if any result would ensue. It was a happy inspiration that induced me to do this, for out of that small beginning has arisen the most interesting correspondence in which I have ever been privileged to engage—a correspondence which, I am happy to say, still promises to continue, and the existence of which, more than any experiences of phenomena which I have had, though the most wonderful of these are yet to be described, is the *raison d'être* of this little book.

The idea I had specially in my mind when I wrote the letter above referred to, was that of all test phenomena one could wish for, the best would be the production in our presence in India of a copy of the London *Times* of that day's date. With such a piece of evidence in my hand, I argued, I would undertake to convert everybody in Simla who was capable of linking two ideas together, to a belief in the possibility of obtaining by occult agency physical results which were beyond the control of ordinary science. I am sorry that I have not kept copies of the letter itself nor of my own subsequent letters, as they would have helped to elucidate the replies in a convenient way; but I did not at the time foresee the developments to which they would give rise and, after all, the interest of the correspondence turns almost entirely on the letters I received: only in a very small degree on those I sent.

A day or two elapsed before I heard anything of the fate of my letter, but Madame Blavatsky then informed me that I was to have an answer. I afterwards learned that she had not been able at first to find a Brother willing to receive the communication. Those whom she first applied to declined to be troubled with the matter. At last her psychological telegraph brought her a favourable answer from one of the Brothers with whom she had not for some time been in communication. He would take the letter and reply to it.

Hearing this, I at once regretted that I had not written at greater length, arguing my view of the required concession more fully. I wrote again, therefore, without waiting for the actual receipt of the expected letter.

A day or two after I found one evening on my writing-table the first letter sent me by my new correspondent. I may here explain, what I learned afterwards, that he was a native of the Punjab who was attracted to occult studies from his earliest boyhood. He was sent to Europe while still a youth at the intervention of a relative—himself an occultist—to be educated in Western knowledge, and since then has been fully initiated in the greater knowledge of the East. From the self complacent point of view of the ordinary European this will seem a strange reversal of the proper order of things, but I need not stop to examine that consideration now.

My correspondent is known to me as the Mahatma Koot Hoomi. This is his "Tibetan Mystic name "—occultists, it would seem, taking new names on initiation—a practice which has no doubt given rise to similar customs which we find perpetuated here and there in ceremonies of the Roman Catholic church.

The letter I received began, *in medias res*, about the phenomenon I had professed. "Precisely," the Mahatma wrote, "because the test of the London newspaper would close the mouths of the sceptics, "it was inadmissible." See it in what light you will, the world is yet in its first stage of disenthralment.... hence unprepared. Very true we work by natural, not supernatural, means and laws. But as on the one hand science would find itself unable, in its present state, to account for the wonders given in its name, and on the other the ignorant masses would still be left to view the phenomenon in the light of a miracle, everyone who would thus be made a witness to the occurrence would be thrown off his balance, and the result would be deplorable. Believe me it would be so especially for yourself, who originated the idea, and for the devoted woman who so foolishly rushes into the wide, open door leading to notoriety. This door, though opened by so friendly a hand as yours, would prove very soon a trap—and a fatal one, indeed, for her. And such is not surely your object...Were we to accede to your desires know you really what consequences would follow in the trail of success? The inexorable shadow which follows all human innovations moves on, yet few are they who are ever conscious of its approach and dangers. What are, then, they to expect who would offer the world an innovation which, owing to human ignorance, if believed in, will surely be attribute to those dark agencies the two-thirds of humanity believe in and dread as yet?.... The success of an attempt of such a kind as the one you propose must be calculated and based upon a thorough knowledge of the people around you. It depends entirely upon the social and moral conditions of the people in their bearing on these deepest and most mysterious questions which can stir the human mind—the deific powers in man and the possibilities contained in Nature. How many even of your best friends, of those who surround you, are more than superficially interested in these abstruse problems? You could count them upon the fingers of your right hand. Your race boasts of having liberated in their century the genius so long imprisoned in the narrow vase of dogmatism and intolerance—the genius of knowledge, wisdom, and free thought. It says that, in their turn, ignorant prejudice and religious bigotry, bottled up like the wicked *djin* of old, and sealed by the Solomons of science, rest at the bottom of the sea, and can never, escaping to the surface again, reign over the world as in the days of old: that the public mind is quite free, in short, and ready to accept any demonstrated truth. Ay, but is it verily so, my respected friend? Experimental knowledge does not quite date from 1662, when Bacon, Robert Boyle, and the. Bishop of Chester transformed under the royal charter their 'invisible college' into a society for the promotion of experimental science. Ages before the Royal Society found itself becoming a reality upon the plan of the 'Prophetic Scheme,' an innate longing for the hidden, a passionate love for, and the study of, Nature, had led men in every generation to try and fathom her secrets deeper than their neighbours did. *Roma ante Romulum fuit* is an axiom taught us in your English schools. The *Vril* of the *Coming Race* was the common property of races now extinct. And as the very existence of those gigantic ancestors of ours is now questioned-though in the Himavats, on the very territory belonging to you, we have a cave full of the skeletons of these giants—and their huge frames, when found, are invariably regarded as isolated freaks of Nature—so the *Vril*, or *akas* as we call it, is looked upon as an impossibility—a myth. And without a thorough knowledge of akas—its combinations and properties, how can science hope to account for such phenomena? We doubt not but the men of your science are open to conviction; yet facts must be first demonstrated to them; they must first have become their own property, have proved amenable to their modes of investigation, before you find them ready to admit them as facts. If you but look into the preface to the *Micrographia*, you will find, in Hookes' suggestions, that the intimate relations of object were of less account in his eyes than their external operation on the senses, and Newton's fine discoveries found in him their greatest opponent. The modern Hookeses are many. Like this learned but ignorant man of old, your modern men of science are less anxious to suggest a physical connection of facts which might unlock for them many an occult force in Nature, as to provide a convenient classification of scientific experiments, so that the most essential quality of a hypothesis is, not that it should be *true*, but only *plausible*, in their opinion.

"So far for science—as much as we know of it. As for human nature in general it is the same now as it was a million of years ago. Prejudice, based upon selfishness, a general unwillingness to give up an established order of things for new modes of life and thought—and occult study requires all that and much more—pride and stubborn resistance to truth, if it but upsets their previous notions of things—such are the characteristics of your age......

What, then, would be the results of the most astounding phenomena supposing we consented to have them produced? However successful, danger would be growing proportionately with success. No choice would soon remain but to go on, ever *crescendo*, or to fall in this endless struggle with prejudice and ignorance, killed by your own weapons. Test after test would be required, and would have to be furnished; every subsequent phenomenon expected to be more marvellous than the preceding one. Your daily remark is, that one cannot be expected to believe unless he becomes an eyewitness. Would the lifetime of a man suffice to satisfy the whole world of sceptics? It may an easy matter to increase the original number of believers at Simla to hundreds and thousands. But what of the hundreds of millions of those who could not be made eyewitnesses? The ignorant, unable to grapple with the invisible operators, might some day vent their rage on the visible agents at work; the higher and educated classes would go on disbelieving, as ever, tearing you to shreds as before. In common with many, you blame us for our great secrecy. Yet we know something of human nature, for the experience of long centuries—ay, ages, has taught us. And we know that so long as science has anything to learn, and a shadow of religious dogmatism lingers in the hearts of the multitude, the world's prejudices have to be conquered step by step, not at a rush. As hoary antiquity had more than one Socrates, so the dim future will give birth to more than one martyr. Enfranchised Science contemptuously turned away her face from the Copernican opinion renewing the theories of Aristarchus Samius, who 'affirmeth that the earth moveth circularly about her own centre', years before the Church sought to sacrifice Galileo as a *holocaust* to the Bible. The ablest mathematician at the Court of Edward VI., Robert Recorde, was left to starve in jail by his colleagues, who laughed at his *Castle of Knowledge*, declaring his discoveries vain fantasies All this is old history, you will think. Verily so, but the chronicles of our modern days do not differ very essentially from their predecessors. And we have but to bear in mind the recent persecutions of mediums in England, the burning of supposed witches and sorcerers in South America, Russia, and the frontiers of Spain, to assure ourselves that the only salvation of the genuine proficient in occult sciences lies in the scepticism of the public: the charlatans and the jugglers are the natural shields of the adepts. The public safety is only ensured by our keeping secret the terrible weapons which might otherwise be used against it, and which, as you have been told, become deadly in the hands of the wicked and selfish."

The remainder of the letter is concerned chiefly with personal matters, and need not be here reproduced. I shall, of course, throughout my quotations from letters, leave out passages which, specially addressed to myself, have no immediate bearing on the public argument. The reader must be fearful to remember, however, as I now most unequivocally affirm, that I shall in no case *alter* one syllable of the passages actually quoted. It is important to make this declaration very emphatically, because the more my readers may be acquainted with India, the less they will be willing to believe, except on the most positive testimony, that the letters from the Mahatma, as I now publish them, have been written by a native of India. That such is the fact, however, is beyond dispute.

I replied to the letter above quoted at some length, arguing, if I remember rightly, that the European mind was less hopelessly intractable than Koot Hoomi represented it. His second letter was as follows:—

"We will be at cross purposes in our correspondence until it has been made entirely plain that occult science has its own methods of research, as fixed and arbitrary as the methods of its antithesis, physical science, are in their way. If the latter has its dicta, so also have the former; and he who would cross the boundary of the unseen world can no more prescribe how he will proceed, than the traveller who tries to penetrate to the inner subterranean recesses of L'Hassa the Blessed could show the way to his guide. The mysteries never were, never can be, put within the reach of the general public, not, at least, until that longed— for day when our religious philosophy becomes universal. At no time have more than a scarcely appreciable minority of men possessed Nature's secret, though multitudes have witnessed the practical evidences of the possibility of their possession. The adept is the rare efflorescence of a generation of inquirers; and to become one, he must obey the inward impulse of his soul, irrespective of the prudential considerations of worldly science or sagacity. Your desire is to be brought to communicate with one of us directly, without the agency of either Madame Blavatsky or any medium. Your idea would be, as I understand it, to obtain such communications, either by letter, as the present one, or by audible words, so as to be guided by one of us in the management, and principally in the instruction of the Society. You seek all this, and yet, as you say yourself, hitherto you have not found sufficient reasons to even give up your modes of life, directly hostile to such modes of communication. This is hardly reasonable. He who would lift up high the banner of mysticism and proclaim its reign near at hand must give the example to others. He must be the first to change his modes of life, and, regarding the study of the occult mysteries as the upper step in the ladder of knowledge, must loudly proclaim it such, despite exact science and the opposition of society. The 'kingdom of Heaven is obtained by force', say the Christian mystics. It is but with armed hand, and ready to either conquer or perish, that the modern mystic can hope to achieve his object.

"My first answer covered, I believe, most of the questions contained in your second and even third letter. Having, then, expressed therein my opinion that the world in general was unripe for any too staggering proof of occult power, there but remains to deal with the isolated individuals who seek, like yourself, to penetrate behind the veil of matter into the "world of primal causes ---- *i.e.*, we need only consider now the cases of yourself and Mr. -----."

I should here explain that one of my friends at Simla, deeply interested with me in the progress of this investigation, had, on reading Koot Hoomi's first letter to me, addressed my correspondent himself. More favourably circumstanced than I, for such an enterprise, he had even proposed to make a complete sacrifice of his other pursuits, to pass away into any distant seclusion, which might he appointed for the purpose, where he might, if accepted as a pupil in occultism, learn enough to return to the world armed with powers which would enable him to demonstrate the realities of spiritual development and the errors of modern materialism, and then devote his life to the task of combating modern incredulity and leading men to a practical comprehension of a better life. I resume the letter:—

"This gentleman also has done me the great honour to address me by name, offering to me a few questions, and stating the conditions upon which he would be willing to work for us seriously. But your motives and aspirations being of diametrically opposite character, and hence leading to different results, I must reply to each of you separately."

"The first and chief consideration in determining us to accept or reject your offer lies in the inner motive which propels you to seek our instruction and, in a certain sense, our guidance; the latter in all cases under reserve, as I understand it, and therefore remaining a question independent of aught else. Now, what are your motives? I may try to define them in their general aspects, leaving details for further consideration. They are—(1) The desire to see positive and unimpeachable proofs that there really are forces in Nature of which science knows nothing; (2) The hope to appropriate them some day—the sooner the better, for you do not like to wait—so as to enable yourself; (*a*) to demonstrate their existence to a few chosen Western minds; (*b*) to contemplate future life as an objective reality built upon the rock of knowledge, not of faith; and (*c*) to finally learn—most important this, among all your motives, perhaps, though the most occult and the best guarded—the whole truth about our lodges and ourselves; to get, in short, the positive assurance that the 'Brothers,' of whom everyone hears so much and sees so little, are rare entities, not fictions of a disordered, hallucinated brain. Such, viewed in their best light, appear to us your motives for addressing me. And in the same spirit do I answer them, hoping that my sincerity will not be interpreted in a wrong way, or attributed to anything like an unfriendly spirit.

"To our minds, then, these motives, sincere and worthy of every serious consideration from the worldly standpoint, appear *selfish*. (You have to pardon me what you might view as crudeness of language, if your desire is that which you really profess—to learn truth and get instruction from us who belong to quite a different world from the one you move in.) They are selfish, because you must be aware that the chief object of the Theosophical Society is not so much to gratify individual aspirations as to serve our fellowmen, and the real value of this term 'selfish,' which may jar upon your ear, has a peculiar significance with us which it cannot have with you; therefore, to begin with, you must not accept it otherwise than in the former sense. Perhaps you will better appreciate our meaning when told that in our view the highest aspirations for the welfare of humanity become tainted with selfishness, if, in the mind of the philanthropist, there lurks the shadow of a desire for self-benefit, or a tendency to do injustice, even where these exist unconsciously to himself. Yet you have ever discussed but to put down, the idea of a Universal Brotherhood, questioned its usefulness, and advised to remodel the Theosophical Society on the principle of a college for the special study of occultism...

"Having disposed of personal motives, let us analyse your terms for helping us to do public good. Broadly stated, these terms are—first, that an independent Anglo-Indian Theosophical Society shall be founded through your kind services, in the management of which neither of our present representatives shall have any voice;[3] And second, that one of us shall take the new body 'under his patronage,' be 'in free and direct communication with its leaders,' and afford them 'direct proof that he really possessed that superior knowledge of the forces of Nature and the attributes of the human soul which would inspire them with proper confidence in his leadership.' I have copied your own words so as to avoid inaccuracy in defining the position.

"From your point of view, therefore, those terms may seem so very reasonable as to provoke no dissent, and, indeed, a majority of your countrymen—if not of Europeans—might share that opinion. What, will you say, can be more reasonable than to ask that that teacher anxious to disseminate his knowledge, and pupil offering him to do so, should be brought face to face, and the one give the experimental proof to the other that his instructions were correct? Man of the world, living in, and in full sympathy with it, you are undoubtedly right. But the men of this other world of ours, untutored in your modes of thought, and, who find it very hard at times to follow and appreciate the latter, can hardly be blamed for not responding as heartily to your suggestions as in your opinion they deserve. The first and most important of our objections is to be found in our *rules*. True, we have our schools and teachers, our neophytes and 'shaberons' (superior adepts) and the door is always opened to the right man who knocks. And we invariably welcome the new comer; only, instead of going over to him, he has to come to us. More than that, unless he has reached that point in the path of occultism from which return is impossible by his having irrevocably pledged himself to our Association, we never except in cases of utmost moment visit him or even cross the threshold of his door in visible appearance.

"Is any of you so eager for knowledge and the beneficent powers it confers, as to be ready to leave your world and come into ours? Then let him come, but he must not think to return until the seal of the mysteries has locked his lips even against the chances of his own weakness or indiscretion. Let him come by all means as the pupil to the master, and without conditions, or let him wait, as so many others have, and be satisfied with such crumbs of knowledge as may fall in his way.

"And supposing you were thus to come, as two of your own countrymen have already—as Madame B. did and Mr. O. wil—supposing you were to abandon all for the truth; to toil wearily for years up the hard, steep road, not daunted by obstacles, firm under every temptation; were to faithfully keep within your heart the secrets entrusted to you as a trial; had worked with all your energies and unselfishly to spread the truth and provoke men to correct thinking and a correct life —would you consider it just, if, after all your efforts, we were to grant to Madame B., or Mr. O. as 'outsiders' the terms you now ask for yourselves. Of these two persons, one has already given three-fourths of a life, the other six years of manhood's prime to us, and both will so labour to the close of their days; though ever working for their merited reward, yet never demanding it, nor murmuring when disappointed. Even though they respectively could accomplish far less then they do, would it not be a palpable injustice to ignore them in an important field of Theosophical effort? Ingratitude is not among our vices, nor do we imagine you would wish to advise it.

"Neither of them has the least inclination to interfere with the management of the contemplated Anglo-Indian Branch, nor dictate its officers. But the new Society, if formed at all, must, though bearing a distinctive title of its own, be, in fact, a branch of the parent body, as is the British Theosophical Society at London, and contribute to its vitality and usefulness by promoting its leading idea of a Universal Brotherhood, and in other practicable ways.

"Badly as the phenomena may have been shown, there have still been, as yourself admit, certain ones that are unimpeachable. The 'raps on the table when no one touches it', and the 'bell sounds in the air,' have, you say, always been regarded as satisfactory, etc. etc. From this, you reason that good test phenomena 'may easily be multiplied *ad infinitum*.' So they can—in any place where our magnetic and other conditions are constantly offered, and where we do not have to act with and through an enfeebled female body, in which, as we might say, a vital cyclone is raging much of the time. But imperfect as may be our visible agent, yet she is the best available at present, and her phenomena have for about half a century astonished and baffled some of the cleverest minds of the age...."

"Two or three little notes which I next received from the Mahatma had reference to an incident I must now describe, the perfection of which as a test phenomenon appears to me more complete than that of any other I have yet described. It is worth notice, by-the-bye, that although the circumstances of this incident were related in the Indian papers at the time, the happy company of scoffers who flooded the Press with their simple comments on the brooch phenomenon, never cared to discuss "the pillow incident."

Accompanied by our guests, we went to have lunch one day on the top of a neighbouring hill, The night before, I had had reason to think that my correspondent, Koot Hoomi, had been in what, for the purpose of the present explanation, I may call subjective communication with me. I do not go into any details, because it is unnecessary to trouble the general reader with impressions of that sort, After discussing the subject in the morning, I found on the hall-table a note from Koot Hoomi, in which he promised to give me something on the hill which should be a token of his (astral) presence near me the previous night.

We went to our destination, camped down on the top of the hill, and were engaged on our lunch, when Madame Blavatsky said Koot Hoomi was asking where we would like to find the object he was going to send me. Let it be understood that up to this moment there had been no conversation in regard to the phenomenon I was expecting. The usual suggestion will, perhaps, be made that Madame Blavatsky "led up" to the choice I actually made. The fact of the matter was simply that in the midst of altogether other talk Madame Blavatsky pricked up her ears on hearing her occult voice—at once told me what was the question asked, and did not contribute to the selection made by one single remark on the subject, In fact, there was no general discussion, and it was by an absolutely spontaneous choice of my own that I said, after a little reflection, "inside that cushion," pointing to one against which one of the ladies present was leaning. I had no sooner uttered the words than my wife cried out, "Oh no, let it be inside mine," or words to that effect. I said, "very well, inside my wife's cushion;" Madame Blavatsky asked the Mahatma by her own methods if that would do, and received an affirmative reply. My liberty of choice as regards the place where the object should be found was thus absolute and unfettered by conditions. The most natural choice for me to have made under the circumstances, and having regard to our previous experiences, would have been up some particular tree, or buried in a particular spot of the ground; but the inside of a sewn-up cushion, fortuitously chosen on the spur of a moment, struck me, as my eye happened to fall upon the cushion I mentioned first, as a particularly good place; and when I had started the idea of a cushion, my wife's amendment to the original proposal was really an improvement, for the particular cushion then selected had never been for a moment out of her own possession all the morning. It was her usual jampan cushion; she had been leaning against it all the way from home, and was leaning against it still, as her jampan had been carried right up to the top of the hill, and she had continued to occupy it. The cushion itself was very firmly made of worsted work and velvet, and had been in our possession for years. It always remained, when we were at home, in the drawing-room, in a conspicuous corner of a certain sofa whence, when my wife went out, it would be taken to her jampan and again brought in on her return.

When the cushion was agreed to, my wife was told to put it under her rug, and she did this with her own hands, inside her jampan. It may have been there about a minute, when Madame Blavatsky said we could set to work to cut it open. I did this with a penknife, and it was a work of some time, as the cushion was very securely sewn all round, and very strongly, so that it had to be cut open almost stitch by stitch, and no tearing was possible. When one side of the cover was completely ripped up, we found that the feathers of the cushion were enclosed in a separate inner case, also sewn round all the edges. There was nothing to be found between the inner cushion and the outer case; so we proceeded to rip up the inner cushion; and this done, my wife searched among the feathers.

The first thing she found was a little three-cornered note, addressed to me in the now familiar handwriting of my occult correspondent. It ran as follows:

"MY DEAR BROTHER,

—This brooch, N°. 2, is placed in this very strange place, simply to show you how very easily a real phenomenon is produced, and how still easier it is to suspect its genuineness. Make of it what you like, even to classing me with confederates.

"The difficulty you spoke of last night with respect to the interchange of our letters, I will try to remove. One of our pupils will shortly visit Lahore and the N. W. P.; and an address will be sent to you which you can always use; unless, indeed, you really would prefer corresponding through -----pillows! Please to remark that the present is not dated from a Lodge, but from a Kashmere valley."

While I was reading this note, my wife discovered, by further search among the feathers, the brooch referred to, one of her own, it very old and very familiar brooch which she generally left on her dressing-table when it was not in use. It would have been impossible to invent or imagine a proof of occult power, in the nature of mechanical proofs, more irresistible and convincing than this incident was for us who had personal knowledge of the various circumstances described. The whole force and significance to us of the brooch thus returned, hinged on to my subjective impressions of the previous night. The reason for selecting the brooch as a thing to give us, dated no earlier than then. On the hypothesis, therefore, idiotic hypothesis as it would be on all grounds, that the cushion must have been got at by Madame Blavatsky, it must have been got at since I spoke of my impressions that morning, shortly after breakfast; but from the time of getting up that morning, Madame Blavatsky had hardly been out of our sight, and had been sitting with my wife in the drawing-room. She had been doing this, by-the-by, against the grain, for she had writing which she wanted to do in her own room, but she had been told by her voices to go and sit in the drawing-room with my wife that morning, and had done so, grumbling at the interruption of her work, and wholly unable to discern any motive for the order. The motive was afterwards clear enough, and had reference to the intended phenomenon. It was desirable that we should have no *arrière pensée* in our minds as to what Madame Blavatsky might possibly have been doing during the morning, in the event of the incident taking such a turn as to make that a factor in determining its genuineness. Of course, if the selection of the pillow could have been foreseen, it would have been unnecessary to victimise our "old Lady," as we generally called her. The presence of the famous pillow itself, with my wife all the morning in the drawing-room, would have been enough. But perfect liberty of choice was to be left to me in selecting a *cache* for the brooch; and the pillow can have been in nobody's mind, any more than in my own, beforehand.

The language of the note given above embodied many little points which had a meaning for us. All through, it bore indirect reference to the conversation that had taken place at our dinner-table the previous evening. I had been talking of the little traces here and there which the long letters from Koot Hoomi bore, showing in spite of their splendid mastery over the language and the vigour of their style, a turn or two of expression that an Englishman would not have made use of; for example, in the form of address, which in the two letters already quoted had been tinged with Orientalism. "But what should he have written?" somebody asked, and I had said, "under similar circumstances an Englishman would probably have written simply: "My dear Brother." Then the allusion to the Kashmir Valley as the place from which the letter was written, instead of from a Lodge, was au allusion to the same conversation; and the underlining of the "k" was another, as Madame Blavatsky had been saying that Koot Hoomi's spelling of "Scepticism" with a "k" was not an Americanism in his case, but due to a philological whim of his.

The incidents of the day were not quite over, even when the brooch was found; for that evening, after we had gone home, there fell from my napkin, after I had unfolded it at dinner, a little note, too private and personal to be reprinted fully, but part of which I am impelled to quote, for the sake of the allusion it contains, to occult *modus operandi*. I must explain that, before starting for the hill, I had penned a few lines of thanks for the promise contained in the note then received as described. This note I gave to Madame Blavatsky, to despatch by occult methods if she had an opportunity. And she carried it in her hand as she and my wife went on in advance, in jampans, along the Simla Mall, not finding an opportunity until about halfway to our destination. Then she got rid of the note, occultism only knows how. This circumstance had been spoken of at the picnic; and as I was opening the note found in the pillow, someone suggested that it would, perhaps, be found to contain an answer to my note just sent. It did not contain any allusion to this, as the reader will be already aware.

The note I received at dinnertime said:—"A few words more. Why should you have felt disappointed at not receiving a direct reply to your last note. It was received in my room about half a minute after the currents for the production of the pillow *dak*, had been set ready, and in full play. And there was no necessity for an answer..."

It seemed to bring one in imagination one step nearer a realisation of the state of the facts to hear "the currents" employed to accomplish what would have been a miracle for all the science of Europe, spoken of thus familiarly.

A miracle for all the science of Europe, and as hard a fact for us, nevertheless, as the room in which we sat. We knew that the phenomenon we had seen was a wonderful reality; that the thought-power of a man in Kashmir had picked up a material object from a table in Simla, and, disintegrating it by some process of which Western science does not yet dream, had passed it through other matter, and had there restored it to its original solidarity, the dispersed particles resuming their precise places as before, and reconstituting the object down to every line or scratch upon its surface. (By-the-by, it bore some scratches when it emerged from the pillow which it never bore before—the initials of our friend.) And we knew that written notes on tangible paper had been flashing backwards and forwards that day between our friend and ourselves, though hundreds of miles of Himalayan mountains intervened between us, and had been flashing backwards and forwards with the speed of electricity, And yet we knew that an impenetrable wall, built up of its own prejudice and obstinacy, of its learned ignorance and polished dulness, was established round the minds of scientific men in the West, as a body, across which we should never be able to carry our facts and our experience. And it is with a greater sense of oppression than people who have never been in a similar position will realise, that I now tell the story I have to tell, and know all the while that the solemn accuracy of its minutest detail, the utter truthfulness of every syllable in this record, is little better than incense to my own conscience —that the scientific minds of the West with which of all cultivated minds my own has hitherto been most in sympathy, will be closed to my testimony most hopelessly. "Though one should rise from the dead," etc.. It is the old story. It is the old story, at all events as regards the crashing results on opinion which such evidence as that I have been giving, ought to have. The smile of incredulity which thinks itself so wise and is so foolish, the suspicions which flatter themselves they are so cunning, and are really the fruit of so much dulness, will gleam over these pages, and wither all their meaning—for the readers who smile. But I suppose that Koot Hoomi is not only right in declaring the world unripe as yet for too staggering a proof of occult power, but also in taking a friendly interest, as it will be seen presently that he does, in the little book I am writing, as one of the influences which bit by bit may sap the foundations of dogmatism and stupidity, on which science, which thinks itself so liberal, has latterly become so firmly rooted.

The next letter—the third long one—that I received from the Mahatma, reached me shortly after my return for the cold weather to Allahabad. But I received one communication from him—a telegram —before its arrival, on the day of my own return to Allahabad. This telegram, of no great importance as regards its contents, which were little more than an expression of thanks for some letters I had written in the papers, was, nevertheless, of great interest indirectly, affording me, as it ultimately did, evidence of a kind which could appeal to other minds besides my own, that Koot Hoomi's letters were not, as some ingenious persons may have been inclined to imagine—in spite of various mechanical difficulties in the way of the theory—the work of Madame Blavatsky. For me, knowing her as intimately as I did, the inherent evidence of the style was enough to make the suggestion that she might have written them, a mere absurdity. And, if it is urged that the authoress of "Isis Unveiled" has certainly a command of language which renders it difficult to say what she could not write, the answer is simple. In the production of this book she was so largely helped by the Brothers, that great portions of it are not really her work at all. She never makes any disguise of this fact, though it is one of a kind which it is useless for her to proclaim to the world at large, as it would be perfectly unintelligible, except to persons who knew something of the external facts, at all events, of occultism. Koot Hoomi's letters, as I say, are perfectly unlike her own style. But, in reference to some of them, receiving them as I did while she was in the house with me, it was not mechanically possible that she might have been the writer. Now, the telegram I received at Allahabad, which was wired to me from Jhelum, was in reply specially to a letter I addressed to Koot Hoomi just before leaving Simla, and enclosed to Madame Blavatsky, who had started some days previously, and was then at Amritsur. She received the letter, with its enclosure, at Amritsur on the 27th of October, as I came to know, not merely from knowing when I sent it, but positively by means of the envelope which she returned to me at Allahabad by direction of Koot Hoomi, not in the least knowing why he wished it sent to me. I did not at first see what on earth was the use of the old envelope to me, but I put it away and afterwards obtained the clue to the idea in Koot Hoomi's mind when Madame Blavatsky wrote me word that he wanted me to obtain the original of the Jhelum telegram. Through the agency of a friend connected with the administration of the telegraph department, I was enabled eventually to obtain a sight of the original of the telegram—a message of about twenty words; and then I saw the meaning of the envelope. The message was in Koot Hoomi's own handwriting, and it was an answer from Jhelum to a letter which the delivery postmark on the envelope showed to have been delivered at Amritsur on the same day the message was sent. Madame Blavatsky assuredly was herself at Amritsur on that date, seeing large numbers of people there in connection with the work of the Theosophical Society, and the handwriting of Koot Hoomi's letters, nevertheless, appears on a telegram undeniably handed in at the Jhelum office on that date. So although some of Koot Hoomi's letters passed through her hands to me, she is proved not to be their writer, as she is certainly not the producer of their handwriting.

Koot Hoomi was probably himself actually at or near Jhelum at the time, as he came down into the midst of the world for a few days, under peculiar circumstances, to see Madame Blavatsky: the letter I received at Allahabad shortly after my return explained this.

Madame Blavatsky had been deeply hurt by the behaviour of some incredulous persons at Simla whom she had met at our house and elsewhere, who, being unable to assimilate the experience they had had of her phenomena, got by degrees into that hostile frame of mind which is one of the phases of feeling I am now used to seeing developed. Perfectly unable to show how the phenomena can be the result of fraud, but thinking that, because they do not understand them, they must be fraudulent, people of a certain temperament become possessed with the spirit which animated persecution by religious authorities in the infancy of physical science. And, by a piece of bad luck, a gentleman who was thus affected was annoyed at a trifling indiscretion on the part of Colonel Olcott, who, in a letter to one of the Bombay papers, quoted some expressions he had made use of in praise of the Theosophical Society and its good influence on the natives. All the irritation thus set up, worked on Madame Blavatsky's excitable temperament to an extent which only those who know her will be able to imagine. The allusions in Koot Hoomi's letter will now be understood. After some reference to important business with which he had been concerned since writing to me last, Koot Hoomi went on:—

"You see, then, that we have weightier matters than small societies to think about; yet the Theosophical Society must not be neglected. The affair has taken an impulse which, if not well guided, might beget very evil issues. Recall to mind the avalanches of your admired Alps, and remember that at first their mass is small, and their momentum little. A trite comparison, you may say, but I cannot think of a better illustration when viewing the gradual aggregation of trifling events growing into a menacing destiny for the Theosophical Society. It came quite forcibly upon me the other day as I was coming down the defiles of Konenlun —Karakorum you call them—and saw an avalanche tumble. I had gone personally to our chief... and was crossing over to Lhadak on my way home. What other speculations might have followed I cannot say. But just as I was taking advantage of the awful stillness which usually follows such cataclysms, to get a clearer view of the present situation, and the disposition of the 'mystics' at Simla, I was rudely recalled to my senses. A familiar voice, as shrill as the one attributed to Saraswati's peacock—which, if we may credit tradition, frightened off the King of the Nagas—shouted along the currents—"Koot Hoomi,........ come quicker and help me!" and, in her excitement, forgot she was speaking English. I must say that the "old Lady's" telegrams do strike one like stones from a catapult.

"What could I do but come. Argument through space with one who was in cold despair and in a state of moral chaos, was useless. So I determined to emerge from a seclusion of many years, and spend some time with her to comfort her as well as I could. But our friend is not one to cause her mind to reflect the philosophical resignation of Marcus Aurelius. The Fates never wrote, that she could say:—'It is a royal thing when one is doing good to hear evil spoken of himself.' I had come for a few days, but now find that I myself cannot endure for any length of time the stifling magnetism even of my own countrymen. I have seen some of our proud old Sikhs drunk and staggering over the marble pavement of their sacred temple. I have heard an English-speaking Vakil declaim against *Yog Vidya* and Theosophy as a delusion and a lie, declaring that English science had emancipated them from such degrading superstitions, and saying that it was an insult to India to maintain that the dirty Yogees and Sunuyasis knew anything about the mysteries of Nature, or that any living man can, or ever could, perform any phenomena. I turn my face homeward tomorrow.

"........I have telegraphed you my thanks for your obliging compliance with my wishes in the matter you allude to in your letter of the 24th..... Received at Amritsur, on the 27th, at 2 P.M. I got your letter about thirty miles beyond Rawul Pinder, five minutes later, and had an acknowledgement wired to you from Jhelum at 4 P. M. on the same afternoon. Our modes of accelerated delivery and quick communications[4] are not, then, as you will see, to be despised by the Western world, or even the Aryan English-speaking and sceptical Vakils.

"I could not ask a more judicial frame of mind in an ally than that in which you are beginning to find yourself. My brother, you have already changed your attitude toward us in a distinct degree. What is to prevent a perfect mutual understanding one day?...... It is not possible that there should be much more at best than a. benevolent neutrality shown by your people towards ours. There is so very minute a point of contact between the two civilisations they respectively represent, that one might almost say they could not touch at all. Nor would they, but for the few —shall I say eccentrics?—who, like you, dream better and bolder dreams than the rest, and, provoking thought, bring the two together by their own admirable audacity."

The letter before me at present is occupied so much with matters personal to myself, that I can only make quotations here and there; but these are specially interesting, as investing with an air of reality subjects which are generally treated in "vague and pompous language. Koot Hoomi was anxious to guard me from idealising the Brothers too much on the strength of my admiration for their marvellous powers.

"Are you certain," he writes, "that the pleasant impression you now may have from our correspondence would not instantly be destroyed upon seeing me. And which of our holy *shaberons* has had the benefit of even the little university education and inkling of European manners that has fallen to my share. An instance: I desired Madame Blavatsky to select, among the two or three Aryian Punjabees who study Yog Vidya and are natural mystics, one whom, without disclosing myself to him too much, I could designate as an agent between yourself and us, and whom I was anxious to despatch to you with a letter of introduction, and have him to speak to you of Yoga and its practical effects. This young gentleman, who is as pure as purity itself, whose aspirations and thoughts are of the most spiritual, ennobling kind, and who, merely through self-exertion, is able to penetrate into the regions of the formless world—this young man is not fit for a drawing-room. Having explained to him that the greatest good might result for his country if he helped you to organise a branch of English mystics, by proving to them practically to what wonderful results led the study of Yog, Madame Blavatsky asked him, in guarded and very delicate terms, to change his dress and turban before starting for Allahabad; for—though she did not give him this reason—they were very dirty and slovenly. You are to tell Mr. Sinnett, she said, that you bring him a letter from the Brother, with whom he corresponds; but if he asks you anything either of him or the other Brothers, answer him simply and truthfully that you are not allowed to expatiate upon the subject. Speak of Yog, and prove to him what powers you have attained. 'This young man who had consented, wrote later on the following curious letter: —'Madame,' he said, 'you who preach the highest standard of morality, of truthfulness, etc., you would have me play the part of an impostor. You ask me to change, my clothes at the risk of giving a false idea of my personality and mystifying the gentleman you send me to. Here is an illustration of the difficulties under which we have to labour. Powerless to send you a neophyte before you have pledged yourself to us, we have to either keep back or despatch to you one who, at best, would shock, if not inspire, you at once with disgust."

The present letter yields only little more that it seems desirable to quote. In a guarded way, Koot Hoomi said that as often as it was practicable to communicate with me, "whether ....by letters (in or out of pillows) or personal visits in astral form, it will be done. But remember," he added, "that Simla is 7,000 feet higher than Allahabad, and the difficulties to be surmounted at the latter are tremendous." To the ordinary mind, feats of " magic " are hardly distinguishable by degrees of difficulty, and the little hint contained in the last sentence may thus help to show that, magical as the phenomena of the Brothers appear (as soon as the dull-witted hypothesis of fraud is abandoned), they are magic of a kind which is amenable to its own laws. Most of the bodies in Nature were elements, in the infancy of chemistry; but in turn the number is reduced by deeper and deeper researches into the law of combinations—and so with magic. To ride the clouds in a basket, or send messages under the sea, would have been magic in one age of the world, but becomes the commonplace of the next. The Simla phenomena are magic for the majority of this generation, but psychological telegraphy itself may become, if not the property of mankind a few generations hence, a fact of science as undeniable as the differential calculus, and known to be attainable by its own appropriate students. That it is easier to accomplish it and cognate achievements, in certain strata of the atmosphere rather than in others, is already a practical suggestion which tends to drag it down from the realms of magic; or, as the same idea might be differently expressed, to lift it towards the region of exact science.

I am here enabled to insert the greater part of a letter addressed by Koot Hoomi to the friend referred to in a former passage, as having opened up a correspondence with him in reference to the idea which he contemplated under certain conditions, of devoting himself entirely to the pursuit of occultism. This letter throws a great deal of light upon some of the metaphysical conceptions of the occultists, and their metaphysics, be it remembered, are a great deal more than abstract speculation.

"DEAR SIR

—Availing of the first moments of leisure to formally answer your letter of the 17th ultimo, I will now report the result of my conference with our chiefs upon the proposition therein contained, trying at the same time to answer all your questions.

"I am first to thank you on behalf of the whole section of our fraternity that is especially interested in the welfare of India for an offer of help whose importance and sincerity no one can doubt. Tracing our lineage through the vicissitudes of Indian civilization from a remote past, we have a love for our motherland no deep and passionate that it has survived even the broadening and cosmopolitanizing (pardon me if that is not an English word) effect of our studies in the laws of Nature. And so I, and every other Indian patriot, feel the strongest gratitude for every kind word or deed that is given in her behalf.

"Imagine, then, that since we are all convinced that the degradation of India is largely due to the suffocation of her ancient spirituality, and that whatever helps to restore that higher standard of thought and morals, must be regenerating in national force, everyone of us would naturally and without urging, be disposed to push forward a society whose proposed formation is under debate, especially if it really is meant to become a society untainted by selfish motive, and whose object is the revival of ancient science, and tendency, to rehabilitate our country in the world's estimation. Take this for granted without further asseverations. But you know, as any man who has read history, that patriots may burst their hearts in vain if circumstances are against them. Sometimes it has happened that no human power, not even the fury and force of the loftiest patriotism, has been able to bend an iron destiny aside from its fixed course, and nations have gone out like torches dropped into the water in the engulfing blackness of ruin. Thus, we who have the sense of our country's fall, though not the power to lift her up at once, cannot do as we would either as to general affairs or this particular one. And with the readiness, but not the right to meet your advances more than half way, we are forced to say that the idea entertained by Mr. Sinnett and yourself is impracticable in part. It is, in a word, impossible for myself or any Brother, or even an advanced neophyte, to be specially assigned and set apart as the guiding spirit or chief of the Anglo-Indian branch. We know it would be a good thing to have you and a few of your colleagues regularly instructed and shown the phenomena and their rationale. For though none but you few would be convinced, still it would be a decided gain to have even a few Englishmen, of first-class ability, enlisted as students of Asiatic Psychology. We are aware of all this, and much more; hence we do not refuse to correspond with, and otherwise help you in various ways. But what we do refuse is, to take any other responsibility upon ourselves than this periodical correspondence and assistance with our advice, and, as occasion favours, such tangible, possibly visible, proofs, as would satisfy you of our presence and interest. To "guide" you we will not consent. However much we may be able to do, yet we can promise only to give you the full measure of your deserts. Deserve much, and we will prove honest debtors; little, and you need only expect a compensating return. This is not a mere text taken from a schoolboy's copybook, though it sounds so, but only the clumsy statement of the law of our order, and we cannot transcend it. Utterly unacquainted with Western, especially English, modes of thought and action, were we to meddle in an organization of such a kind, you would find all your fixed habits and traditions incessantly clashing, if not with the new aspirations themselves, at least with their modes of realisation as suggested by us. You could not get unanimous consent to go even the length you might yourself. I have asked Mr. Sinnett to draft a plan embodying your joint ides for submission to our chiefs, this seeming the shortest way to a mutual agreement. Under our 'guidance' your branch could not live, you not being men to be guided at all in that sense.—Hence the society would be a premature birth and a failure, looking as incongruous as a Paris Daumont drawn by a team of Indian yaks or camels. You ask us to teach you true science—the occult aspect of the known side of Nature; and this you think can be as easily done as asked. You do not seem to realise the tremendous difficulties in the way of imparting even the rudiments of *our* science to those who have been trained in the familiar methods of yours. You do not see that the more you have of the one the less capable you are of instinctively comprehending the other, for a man can only think in his worn grooves, and unless he has the courage to fill up these, and make new ones for himself, he must perforce travel on the old lines. Allow me a few instances. In conformity with exact science you would define but one cosmic energy, and see no difference between the energy expended by the traveller who pushes aside the bush that obstructs his path, and the scientific experimenter who expends an equal amount of energy in setting a pendulum in motion. We do; for we know there is a world of difference between the two. The one uselessly dissipates and scatters force, the other concentrates and stores it. And here please understand that I do not refer to the relative utility of the two, as one might imagine, but only to the fact that in the one case there is but brute force flung out without any transmutation of that brute energy into the higher potential form of spiritual dynamics, and in the other there is just that. Please do not consider me vaguely metaphysical. The idea I wish to convey is that the result of the highest intellection in the scientifically occupied brain is the evolution of a sublimated form of spiritual energy, which, in the cosmic action, is productive of illimitable results; while the automatically acting brain holds, or stores up in itself, only a certain quantum of brute force that is unfruitful of benefit for the individual or humanity. The human brain is an exhaustless generator of the most refined quality of cosmic force out of the low, brute energy of Nature; and the complete adept has made himself a centre from which irradiate potentialities that beget correlations upon correlations through Aeons of time to come. This is the key to the mystery of his being able to project into and materialise in the visible world the forms that his imagination has constructed out of inert cosmic matter in the invisible world. The adept does not create anything new, but only utilizes and manipulates materials which Nature has in store around him, and material which, throughout eternities, has passed through all the forms. He has but to choose the one he wants, and recall it into objective existence. Would not this sound to one of your 'learned' biologists like a madman's dream?

"You say there are few branches of science with which you do not possess more or less acquaintance, and that you believe you are doing a certain amount of good having acquired the position to do this by long years of study. Doubtless you do; but will you permit me to sketch for you still more clearly the difference between the modes of physical (called exact out of mere compliment) and metaphysical sciences. The latter, as you know, being incapable of verification before mixed audiences, is classed by Mr. Tyndall with the fictions of poetry. The realistic science of fact on the other hand is utterly prosaic. Now, for us, poor unknown philanthropists, no fact of either of these sciences is interesting except in the degree of its potentiality of moral results, and in the ratio of its usefulness to mankind. And what, in its proud isolation, can be more utterly indifferent to everyone and everything, or more bound to nothing but the selfish requisites for its advancement, then, this materialistic science of fact? May I ask then, what have the laws of Faraday, Tyndall, or others to do with philanthropy in their abstract relations with humanity, viewed as an intelligent whole? What care they for *Man* as an isolated atom of this great and harmonious whole, even though they may be sometimes of practical use to him? Cosmic energy is something eternal and incessant; matter is indestructible and there stand the scientific facts. Doubt them, and you are an ignoramus; deny them, a dangerous lunatic, a bigot; pretend to improve upon the theories—an impertinent charlatan. And yet even these scientific facts never suggested any proof to the word of experimenters that Nature consciously prefers that matter should be indestructible under organic rather than inorganic forms, and that she works slowly but incessantly towards the realisation of this object—the evolution of conscious life out of inert material. Hence, their ignorance about the scattering and concretion of cosmic energy in its metaphysical aspects, their division about Darwin's theories, their uncertainty about the degree of conscious life in separate elements, and, as a necessity, the scornful rejection of every phenomenon outside their own stated conditions, and the very idea of worlds of semi-intelligent if not intellectual forces at work in hidden corners of Nature. To give you another practical illustration—we see a vast difference between the two qualities of two equal amounts of energy expended by two men, of whom one, let us suppose, is on his way to his daily quiet work, and another on his way to denounce a fellow creature at the police-station, while the men of science see none; and we—not they—see a specific difference between the energy in the motion of the wind and that of a revolving wheel. And why? Because every thought of man upon being evolved passes into the inner world, and becomes an active entity by associating itself, coalescing we might term it, with an elemental—that is to say, with one of the semi-intelligent forces of the kingdoms. It survives as an active intelligence—a creature of the mind's begetting—for a longer or shorter period proportionate with the original intensity of the cerebral action which generated it. Thus, a good thought is perpetuated as an active, beneficent power, an evil one as a maleficent demon. And so man is continually peopling his current in space with a world of his own, crowded with the offsprings of his fancies, desires, impulses, and passions; a current which reacts upon any sensitive or nervous organization which comes in contact with it, in proportion to its dynamic intensity. The Buddhist calls this his 'Skandha'; the Hindu gives it the name of 'Karma.' The adept evolves these shapes consciously; other men throw them off unconsciously. The adept, to be successful and preserve his power, must dwell in solitude, and more or less within his own soul. Still less does exact science perceive that while the building ant, the busy bee, the nidifacient bird, accumulates each in its own humble way as much cosmic energy in its potential form as a Haydn, a Plato, or a ploughman turning his furrow, in theirs; the hunter who kills game for his pleasure or profit, or the positivist who applies his intellect to proving that + x + = ---, are wasting and scattering energy no less than the tiger which springs upon its prey. They all rob Nature instead of enriching her, and will all, in the degree of their intelligence, find themselves accountable.

"Exact experimental science has nothing to do with morality, virtue, philanthropy—therefore, can make no claim upon our help until it blends itself with metaphysics. Being but a cold classification of facts outside man, and existing before and after him, her domain of usefulness ceases for us at the outer boundary of these facts; and whatever the inferences and results for humanity from the materials acquired by her method, she little cares. Therefore, as our sphere lies entirely outside hers—as far as the path of Uranus is outside the Earth's—we distinctly refuse to be broken on any wheel of her construction. Heat is but a mode of motion to her, and motion develops heat, but why the mechanical motion of the revolving wheel should be metaphysically of a higher value than the heat into which it is gradually transformed she has yet to discover. The philosophical and transcendental: (hence absurd) notion of the mediaeval Theosophist that the final progress of human labour, aided by the incessant discoveries of man, must one day culminate in a process which, in imitation of the sun energy—in its capacity as a direct motor—shall result in the evolution of nutritious food out inorganic matter, is unthinkable for men of science. Were the sun, the great nourishing father of or planetary system, to hatch granite chickens out of a boulder 'under test conditions' tomorrow, the (the men of science) would accept it as a scientific fact without wasting a regret that the fowls were not alive so as to feed the hungry and the starving. But let a *shaberon* cross the Himalayas in a time of famine and multiply sacks of rice for the perishing multitudes—as he could—and your magistrates and collectors would probably lodge him in jail make him confess what granary he had robbed. This is exact science and your realistic world. An though, as you say, you are impressed by the vast extent of the world's ignorance on every subject which you pertinently designate as a 'few palpable facts collected and roughly generalised, and a technical jargon invented to hide man's ignorance of all that lies behind these facts,' and though you speak of your faith in the infinite possibilities of Nature, yet you are content to spend your life in a work which aids only that same exact science.....

"Of your several questions we will first discuss, if you please, the one relating to the presumed failure of the 'Fraternity' to 'leave any mark upon the history of the world.' They ought, you think, to have been able, with their extraordinary advantages, to have 'gathered into their schools a considerable portion of the more enlightened minds of every race.' How do you know they have made no such mark? Are you acquainted with their efforts, successes, and failures? Have you any dock upon which to arraign them? How could your world collect proofs of the doings of men who have sedulously kept closed every possible door of approach by which the inquisitive would spy upon them? The prime condition of their success was that they should never be supervised or obstructed. What they have done they know; all that those outside their circle could perceive was results, the causes of which were masked from view. To account for these results, men have, in different ages, invented theories of the interposition of gods, special providences, fates, the benign or hostile influence of the stars. There never was a time within or before the so-called historical period when our predecessors were not moulding events and 'making history,' the facts of which were subsequently and invariably distorted by historians to suit contemporary prejudices. Are you quite sure that the visible heroic figures in the successive dramas were not often but their puppets? We never pretended to be able to draw nations in the mass to this or that crisis in spite of the general drift of the world's cosmic relations. The cycles must run their rounds. Periods of mental and moral light and darkness succeed each other as day does night. The major and minor yugas must be accomplished according to the established order of things. And we, borne along on the mighty tide, can only modify and direct some of its minor currents. If we had the powers of the imaginary Personal God, and the universal and immutable laws were but toys to play with, then, indeed, might we have created conditions that would have turned this earth into an arcadia for lofty souls. But having to deal with an immutable law, being ourselves its creatures, we have had to do what we could, and rest thankful. There have been times when a considerable portion of 'enlightened minds' were taught in our schools. Such times there were in India, Persia, Egypt, Greece, and Rome. But, as I remarked in a letter to Mr. Sinnett, the adept is the efflorescence of his age, and comparatively few ever appear in a single century. Earth is the battleground of moral no less than of physical forces, and the boisterousness of animal passion, under the stimulus of the rude energies of the lower group of etheric agents, always tends to quench spirituality. What else could one expect of men so nearly related to the lower kingdom from which they evolved? True also, our numbers are just now diminishing, but this is because, as I have said, we are of the human race, subject to its cyclic impulse, and powerless to turn that back upon itself. Can you turn the Gunga or the Bramaputra back to its sources; can you even dam it so that its piled-up waters will not overflow the banks? No; but you may draw the stream partly into canals, and utilise its hydraulic power for the good of mankind. So we, who cannot stop the world from going in its destined direction, are yet able to divert some part of its energy into useful channels. Think of us as demigods, and my explanation will not satisfy you; view us as simple men—perhaps a little wiser as the result of special study—and it ought to answer your objection.

"What good,' you say, 'is to be attained for my fellows and myself (the two are inseparable) by these occult sciences?' When the natives see that an interest is taken by the English, and even by some high officials in India, in their ancestral science and philosophies, they will themselves take openly to their study. And when they come to realise that the old 'divine' phenomena were not miracles, but scientific effects, superstition will abate. Thus, the greatest evil that now oppresses and retards the revival of Indian civilization will in time disappear. The present tendency of education is to make them materialistic and root out spirituality. With a proper understanding of what their ancestors meant by their writings and teachings, education would become a blessing, whereas now it is often a curse. At present the non-educated, as much as the learned natives, regard the English as too prejudiced, because of their Christian religion and modern science, to care to understand them or their traditions. They mutually hate and mistrust each other. This changed attitude towards the older philosophy, would influence the native princes and wealthy men to endow normal schools for the education of pundits; and old MSS., hitherto buried out of the reach of the Europeans, would again come to light, and with them the key to much of that which was hidden for ages from the popular understanding, for which your sceptical Sanscritists do not care, which your religious missionaries do not *dare*, to understand. Science would gain much, humanity everything. Under the stimulus of the Anglo-Indian Theosophical Society, we might in time see another golden age of Sanskrit literature.....

"If we look at Ceylon we shall see the most scholarly priests combining, under the lead of the Theosophical Society, in a new exegesis of Buddhistic philosophy; and at Galle, on the 15th of September, a secular Theosophical School for the teaching of Singhalese youth, opened with an attendance of over three hundred scholars; an example about to be imitated at three other points in that island. If the Theosophical Society, as at present constituted,' has indeed no 'real vitality,' and yet in its modest way has done so much practical good, how much greater results might not be anticipated from a body organised upon the better plan you could suggest?

"The same causes that are materialising the Hindu mind are equally affecting all Western thought. Education enthrones scepticism, but imprisons spirituality. You can do immense good by helping to give the Western nations a secure basis upon which to reconstruct their crumbling faith. And what they need is the evidence that Asiatic psychology alone supplies. Give this, and you will confer happiness of mind on thousands. The era of blind faith is gone; that of inquiry is here. Inquiry that only unmasks error, without discovering anything upon which the soul can build, will but make iconoclasts. Iconoclasm, from its very destructiveness, can give nothing; it can only raze. But man cannot rest satisfied with bare negation. Agnosticism is but a temporary halt. This is the moment to guide the recurrent impulse which must soon come, and which will push the age towards extreme atheism, or drag it back to extreme sacerdotalism, if it is not led to the primitive soul-satisfying philosophy of the Aryans. He who observes what is going on today, on the one hand among the Catholics, who are breeding miracles as fast as the white ants do their young, on the other among the freethinkers, who are converting, by masses, into Agnostics

—will see the drift of things. The age is revelling at a debauch of phenomena. The same marvels that the spiritualists quote in opposition to the dogmas of eternal perdition and atonement, the Catholics swarm to witness as proof of their faith in miracles. The sceptics make game of both. All are blind and there is no one to lead them. You and your colleagues may help to furnish the materials for a needed universal religious philosophy; one impregnable to scientific assault, because itself the finality of absolute science, and a religion that is indeed worthy of the name since it includes the relations of man physical to man psychical, and of the two to all that is above and below them. Is not this worth a slight sacrifice? And if, after reflection, you should decide to enter this new career, let it be known that your society is no miracle-mongering or banqueting club, nor specially given to the study of phenomenalism. Its chief aim is to extirpate current superstitions and scepticism, and from long-sealed ancient fountains to draw the proof that man may shape his own future destiny, and know for a certainty that he can live hereafter, if he only wills, and that all 'phenomena', are but manifestations of natural law, to try to comprehend which is the duty of every intelligent being."

I have hitherto said nothing of the circumstances under which these various letters reached my hands; nor, in comparison with the intrinsic interest of the ideas they embody, can the phenomenal conditions under which some of them were delivered, be regarded as otherwise than of secondary interest for readers who appreciate their philosophy. But every bit of evidence which helps to exhibit the nature of the powers which the adepts exercise, is worth attention, while the rationale of such powers is still hidden from the world. The fact of their existence can only be established by the accumulation of such evidence, as long as we are unable to prove their possibility by a *priori* analysis of the latent capacities in man.

My friend to whom the last letter was addressed wrote a long reply, and subsequently an additional letter for Koot Hoomi, which he forwarded to me, asking me to read and then seal it up and send or give it to Madame Blavatsky for transmission, she being expected at about that time at my house at Allahabad on her way down country from Amritsur and Lahore, where, as I have already indicated, she had stayed for some little time after our household broke up for the season at Simla. I did as desired, and gave the letter to Madame Blavatsky, after gumming and sealing the stout envelope in which it was forwarded. That evening, a few hours afterwards, on returning home to dinner, I found that the letter had gone, and had come back again.

Madame Blavatsky told me that she had been talking to a visitor in her own room, and had been fingering a blue pencil on her writing-table without noticing what she was doing, when she suddenly noticed that the paper on which she was scribbling was my letter that the addressee had duly taken possession of, by his own methods, an hour or two before. She found that she had, while talking about something else, unconsciously written on the envelope the words which it then bore, "Read and returned with thanks, and a few commentaries. Please open." I examined the envelope carefully, and it was absolutely intact, its very complete fastenings having remained just as I arranged them. Slitting it open, I found the letter which it had contained when I sent it, and another from Koot Hoomi to me, criticising the former with the help of a succession of pencil figures that referred to particular passages in the original letter—another illustration of the passage of matter through matter, which, for thousands of people who have had personal experience of it in Spiritualism, is as certain a fact of nature as the rising of the sun, and which I have now not only encountered at spiritual *séances*, but, as this record will have shown, on many occasions when there is no motive for suspecting any other agency than that of living beings with faculties of which we may all possess the undeveloped germs, though it is only in their case that knowledge has brought these to phenomenal fruition.

Sceptical critics, putting aside the collateral bearing of all the previous phenomena I have described, and dealing with this letter incident by itself alone, will perhaps say—of course Madame Blavatsky had ample time to open the envelope by such means as the mediums who profess to get answers to sealed letters from the spirit world are in the habit of employing. But, firstly, the Jhelum telegram proof, and the inherent evidence of the whole correspondence show that, the letters which come to me in that which I recognise as Koot Hoomi's handwriting, are not the work of Madame Blavatsky, at all events; secondly, let the incident I have just described be compared with another illustration of an exactly similar incident which occurred shortly afterwards under different circumstances Koot Hoomi had sent me a letter addressed to my friend to read and forward on. On the subject of this letter before sending it I had occasion to make a communication to Koot Hoomi . I wrote a note to him, fastened it up in an ordinary adhesive envelope, and gave it to Madame Blavatsky. She put it in her pocket, went into her own room, which opened out of the drawing room, and came out again almost instantly. Certainly she had not been away thirty seconds. She said "he" had taken it at once. Then she followed me back through the house to my office room, spoke for a few minutes in the adjoining room to my wife, and, returning into my office, lay down on a couch. I went on with my work, and perhaps ten minutes elapsed, perhaps less. Suddenly she got up. "There's your letter," she said, pointing to the pillow from which she had lifted her head; and there lay the letter I had just written, intact as regards its appearance, but with Koot Hoomi's name on the outside scored out and mine written over it. After a thorough examination I slit the envelope, and found inside, on the flyleaf of my note, the answer I required in Koot Hoomi's handwriting. Now, except for the thirty seconds during which she retired to her own room, Madame Blavatsky had not been out of my sight, except for a minute or two in my wife's room, during the short interval which elapsed between the delivery of the letter by me to her and its return to me as described. And during this interval no one else had come into my room. The incident was as absolute and complete a mechanical proof of abnormal power exercised to produce the result as any conceivable test could have yielded. Except by declaring that I cannot be describing it correctly, the most resolute partisan of the commonplace will be unable seriously to dispute the force of this incident. He may take refuge in idiotic ridicule, or he may declare that I am misrepresenting the facts. As regards the latter hypothesis I can only pledge my word, as I do hereby, to the exact accuracy of the statement.

In one or two cases I have got back answers from Koot Hoomi to my letters in my own envelopes, these remaining intact as addressed to him, but with the address changed, and my letter gone from the inside, his reply having taken its place. In two or three cases I have found short messages from Koot Hoomi written across the blank parts of letters from other persons, coming to me through the post, the writers in these cases being assuredly unaware of the additions so made to their epistles.

Of course I have asked Koot Hoomi for an explanation of these little phenomena, but it is easier for me to ask than for him to answer, partly because the forces which the adepts bring to bear upon matter to achieve abnormal results, are of a kind which ordinary science knows so little about that we of the outer world are not prepared for such explanations; and partly because the manipulation of the forces employed has to do, sometimes, with secrets of initiation which an occultist must not reveal. However, in reference to the subject before us, I received on one occasion this hint as an explanation.

"..........Besides, bear in mind that these my letters are not written, but *impressed*, or precipitated, and then all mistakes corrected."

Of course I wanted to know more about such precipitation; was it a process which followed thought more rapidly than any with which we were familiar? And as regards letters received, did the meaning of these penetrate the understanding of an occult recipient at once, or were they read in the ordinary way?

"Of course I have to read every word you write," Koot Hoomi replied, "otherwise I would make a fine mess of it. And whether it be through my physical or spiritual eyes, the time required for it is practically the same. As much may be said of my replies; for whether I precipitate or dictate them or write my answers myself, the difference in time saved is very minute. I have to think it over, to photograph every word and sentence carefully in my brain, before it can be repeated by precipitation. As the fixing on chemically prepared surfaces of the images formed by the camera requires a previous arrangement within the focus of the object to be represented, for otherwise—as often found in bad photographs—the legs of the sitter might appear out of all proportion with the head, and so on—so we have to first arrange our sentences and impress every letter to appear on paper in our minds before it becomes fit to be read. For the present it is *all* I can tell you. When science will have learned more about the mystery of the lithophyl (or litho-biblion), and how the impress of leaves comes originally to take place on stones, then I will be able to make you better understand the process. But you must know and remember one thing—we but follow and servilely copy Nature in her works."

In another letter Koot Hoomi expatiates more fully on the difficulty of making occult explanations intelligible to minds trained only in modern science.

"Only the progress one makes in the study of arcane knowledge from its rudimental elements brings him gradually to understand our meaning. Only thus, and not otherwise, does it, strengthening and refining those mysterious links of sympathy between intelligent men—the temporarily isolated fragments of the universal soul, and the cosmic soul itself—bring them into full rapport. Once this established, then only will those awakened sympathies serve, indeed, to connect *Man* with—what, for the want of a European scientific word more competent to express the idea, I am again compelled to describe as that energetic chain which binds together the material and immaterial kosmos—Past, Present, and Future, and quicken his perceptions so as to clearly grasp not merely all things of matter, but of spirit also. I feel even irritated at having to use the three clumsy words—Past, Present, and

Future. Miserable concepts of the objective phases of the subjective whole, they are about as ill adapted for the purpose, as an axe for fine carving. Oh, my poor disappointed friend, that you were already so far advanced on THE PATH that this simple transmission of ideas should not be encumbered by the conditions of matter, the union of your mind with ours prevented by its induced incapabilities. Such is unfortunately the inherited and self-acquired grossness of the Western mind, and so greatly have the very phrases expressive of modern thoughts been developed in the line of practical materialism, that it is now next to impossible, either for them to comprehend or for us to express in their own languages anything of that delicate, seemingly ideal, machinery of the occult kosmos. To some little extent that faculty can be acquired by the Europeans through study and meditation, but— that's all. And here is the bar which has hitherto prevented a conviction of the theosophical truths from gaining currency among Western nations—caused theosophical study to be cast aside as useless and fantastic by Western philosophers. How shall I teach you to read and write, or even comprehend a language off which no alphabet palpable or words audible to you have yet been invented. How could the phenomena of our modern electrical science be explained to --- say a "Greek philosopher of the days of Ptolemy, were he suddenly recalled to life—with such an unbridged hiatus in discovery as would exist between his and our age? Would not the very technical terms be to him an unintelligible jargon, an abracadabra of meaningless sounds, and the very instruments and apparatuses used but miraculous monstrosities? And suppose for one instant I were to describe to you the lines of those colour rays that lie beyond the so-called visible spectrum-rays invisible to all but a very few even among us; to explain how we can find in space anyone of the so called subjective or *accidental* colours— the *complement* (to speak mathematically) *moreover' of any other given colour of a dichromatic body* (which alone sounds like an absurdity) could you comprehend, do you think, their optical effect, or even my meaning? And since you see them not—such rays—nor can know them, nor have you any names for them as yet in science, if I were to tell you......'without moving from your writing-desk, try search for, and produce before your eyes the whole solar spectrum decomposed into fourteen prismatic colour—(seven being complementary) as it is but with the help of that occult light that you can see me from a distance as I see you'—what think you would be your answer? What would you have to reply? Would you not be likely enough to retort by telling me that as there never, were but seven (now three) primary colours which, moreover, have never yet by any known physical process been seen decomposed further than the seven prismatic hues, my invitation was as unscientific as it was absurd? Adding that my offer to search for an imaginary solar complement, being no compliment to your knowledge of physical science—I had better, perhaps, go and search for my mythical dichromatic and solar 'pairs' in Tibet, for modern science has hitherto been unable to bring under any theory even so simple a phenomenon as the colours of all such dichromatic bodies. And yet truth knows these colours are objective enough.

"So you see the insurmountable difficulties in the way of obtaining not only *absolute*, but even primary knowledge in Occult Science, for one situated as you are. How could you make yourself understood, *command* in fact, those semi-intelligent forces, whose means of communicating with us are not through spoken words, but through sounds and colours in correlations between the vibrations of the two? For sound, light, and colour are the main factors in forming those grades of intelligences, these beings of whose very existence you have no conception, nor are you allowed to believe in them—Atheists and Christians, Materialists and Spiritualists, all bringing forward their respective arguments against such a belief-Science objecting stronger than either of these to such a degrading superstition.

"Thus, because they cannot with one leap over the boundary walls attain to the pinnacles of Eternity—because we cannot take a savage from the centre of Africa and make him comprehend at once the 'Principia' of Newton, or the 'Sociology' of Herbert Spencer, or make an unlettered child write a new "Iliad in old Achaian Greek, or an ordinary painter depict scenes in Saturn, or sketch the inhabitants of Arcturus—*because if all this our very existence is denied*. Yes, for this reason are believers in us pronounced impostors and fools, and the very science which leads to the highest goal of the highest knowledge, to the real tasting of the Tree of Life and Wisdom—is scouted as a wild flight of imagination."

The following passage occurs in another letter, but it adheres naturally enough to the extract just concluded.

"The truths and mysteries of occultism constitute, indeed, a body of the highest spiritual importance, at once profound and practical for the world at large. Yet it is not as an addition to the tangled mass of theory or speculation that they are being given to you, but for their practical bearing on the interests of mankind. The terms Unscientific, Impossible, Hallucination, Imposture, have hitherto been used in a very loose, careless way, as implying in the occult phenomena something either mysterious and abnormal, or a premeditated imposture. And this is why our chiefs have determined to shed upon a few recipient minds more light upon the subject, and to prove to them that such manifestations are as reducible to law as the simplest phenomena in the physical universe. The wiseacres say, 'the age of miracles is past', but we answer, 'it never existed.' While not unparalleled or without their counterpart in universal history, these phenomena must and *will* come with an overpowering influence upon the world of sceptics and bigots. They *have* to prove both destructive and constructive-destructive in the pernicious errors of the past, in the old creeds and superstitions which suffocate in their poisonous embrace, like the Mexican weed, nigh all mankind; but constructive of new institutions of a genuine, practical Brotherhood of Humanity, where all will become co-workers of Nature, will work for the good of mankind, *with* and *through* the higher *planetary spirits*, the only spirits we believe in. Phenomenal elements previously unthought of, undreamed of, will soon begin manifesting themselves day by day with constantly augmented force, and disclose at last the secrets of their mysterious workings. Plato was right. Ideas rule the world; and as men's minds will receive new ideas, leaving aside the old and effete, the world will advance, mighty revolutions will spring from them, creeds and even powers will crumble before their onward march, crushed by their Irresistible force. It will be just as impossible to resist their influence when the time comes as to stay the progress of the tide. But all this will come gradually on, and before it comes we have a duty set before us: that of sweeping away as much as possible the dross left to us by our pious forefathers. New ideas have to be planted on clean places, for these ideas touch upon the most momentous subjects. It is not physical phenomena, but these universal ideas, that we study; as to comprehend the former, we have first to understand the latter. They touch man's true position in the universe in relation to his previous and future births, his origin and ultimate destiny; the relation of the mortal to the immortal, of the temporary to the eternal, of the finite to the infinite; ideas larger, grander, more comprehensive, recognising the eternal reign of immutable law, unchanging and unchangeable, in regard to which there is only an ETERNAL Now; while to uninitiated mortals, time is past or future, as related to their finite existence on this material speck of dirt. This is what we study and what many have solved........ Meanwhile, being human, I have to rest. I took no sleep for over sixty hours."

Here are It few lines from Koot Hoomi's hand, in a letter not addressed to me, It fall conveniently into the present series of extracts.

"Be it as it may, we are content to live as we do, unknown and undisturbed by a civilization which rests so exclusively upon intellect. Nor do we feel in any way concerned about the revival of our ancient art and high civilization, for these are as sure to come back in their time, and in a higher form, as the Plesiosaurus and the Megatherium in theirs. We have the weakness to believe in ever-recurrent cycles, and hope to quicken the resurrection of what is past and gone. We could not impede it, even if we would. The new civilization will be but the child of the old one, and we have but to leave the eternal law to take its own course, to have our dead ones come out of their graves; yet we are certainly anxious to hasten the welcome event. Fear not, although we do 'cling superstitiously to the relics of the past', our knowledge will not pass away from the sight of man. It is, the 'gift of the gods,' and the most precious relic of all. The keepers of the sacred light did not safely cross so many ages but to find themselves wrecked on the rocks of modern scepticism. Our pilots are too experienced sailors to allow us to fear any such disaster. We will always find volunteers to replace the tired sentries, and the world, bad as it is in its present state of transitory period, can yet furnish us with a few men now and then."

Turning back to my own correspondence, and to the latest letter I received from Koot Hoomi before leaving India on the trip home during which I am writing these pages, I read:—

"I hope that at least *you* will understand that we (or most of us) are far from being the heartless morally dried-up mummies some would fancy us to be. Mejnour is very well where he is—as an ideal character of a thrilling, in many respects truthful story. Yet, believe me, few of us would care to play the part in life of a desiccated pansy between the leaves of a volume of solemn poetry. We may not be quite 'the boys' to quote ——'s irreverent expression when speaking of us, yet none of *our* degree are like the stern hero of Bulwer's romance. While the facilities of observation secured to some of us by our condition certainly give a greater breadth of view, a more pronounced and impartial, a more widely spread humaneness—for answering Addison, we might justly maintain that *it is* the business of "magic" to humanize our natures with compassion'—for the whole mankind as all living beings, instead of concentrating and limiting our affections to one predilected race— yet few of us (except such as have attained the final negation of Moksha) can so far enfranchise ourselves from the influence of our earthly connection as to be unsusceptible in various degrees to the higher pleasures, emotions, and interests of the common run of humanity. Of course the greater the progress towards deliverance, the less this will be the case, until, to crown all, human and purely individual personal feelings, blood-ties and friendship, patriotism and race predilection, will all give way to become blended into one universal feeling, the only true and holy, the only unselfish and eternal one-Love, an Immense Love for humanity as a whole. For it is humanity which is the great orphan, the only disinherited one upon this earth, my friend. And it is the duty of every man who is capable of an unselfish impulse to do something, however little, for its welfare. It reminds me of the old fable of the war between the body and its members; here, too, each limb of this huge 'orphan,' fatherless and motherless, selfishly cares but for itself, The body, uncared for, suffers eternally whether the limbs are at war or at rest. Its suffering and agony never cease; and who can blame it—as your materialistic philosophers do—if, in this everlasting isolation and neglect, it has evolved gods into whom 'it ever cries for help, but is not heard.' Thus—

> *'Since there is hope for man only in man,*
> *I would not let one cry whom I could save.'*

Yet I confess that I individually am not yet exempt from some of the terrestrial attachments. I am still attracted toward some men more than towards others, and philanthropy as preached by our great Patron

> *'..................The Saviour of the world,*
> *The teacher of Nirvana and the Law '*

has never killed in me either individual preferences of friendship, love for my next of kin, or the ardent feeling of patriotism for the country in which I was last materially individualised."

I had asked Koot Hoomi how far I was at liberty to use his letters in the preparation of this volume, and, a few lines after the passage just quoted, he says:—

"I lay no restrictions upon your making use of anything I may have written to you or Mr. ----- having full confidence in your tact and judgment as to what should be printed, and how it should be presented. I must only ask you..." and then he goes on to indicate one letter which he wishes me to withhold...... "As to the rest, I relinquish it to the mangling tooth of criticism."

1. This house at which the cigarette was found was Mr. O'Meara's. He is quite willing that this should be stated.
2. The theory is that a current of what can only be called magnetism, can be made to convey objects, previously dissipated by the same force, to any distance, and in spite of the Intervention of any amount of matter.
3. In the absence of my own letter, to which this Is a reply, the reader might think from this sentence that I had been animated by some unfriendly feeling for the representatives referred to—Madame Blavatsky and Colonel Olcott. This is far from having been the case; but, keenly alive to mistakes which had been made up to the time of, which I am writing, In the management of the Theosophical Society, Mr. ------and myself were under the impression that better public results might be obtained by commencing operations *de novo*, and taking, ourselves, the direction of the measures which might be employed to recommend the study of occultism to the modern world. This belief on our part was coexistent In both cases with a warm friendship based on the purest esteem for both the persons mentioned.
4. Many old Indians, and some books about the Indian Mutiny, take note of the perfectly incomprehensible way news of events transpiring at a distance would sometimes be found to have penetrated the native bazaars before It had reached the Europeans at such places by the quickest means of communication at their disposal. The explanation I have been informed, Is that the Brothers, who were anxious to save the British power at that time, regarding it as a better government for India than any system of native rule that could take its place, were quick to distribute information by their own methods when this could operate to quiet popular excitement and discourage new risings. The sentiment that animated them then, animates them still, and the influence of the Theosophical Society In India is one which the Government would do wisely to countenance and support. The suspicions directed against its founders in the first instance, misdirected as they were, were excusable enough, but now that the character of the whole movement is better understood, it would be well for the officers of the British Government in India who have any opportunity of the kind, to do whatever they can towards showing their sympathy with the promoters of the Society, who must, necessarily, have an uphill task to perform without such manifestations of sympathy.

TEACHINGS OF OCCULT PHILOSOPHY

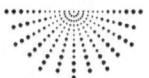

AS AFFIRMED more than once already, Occult Philosophy in various countries and through different periods has remained substantially the same. At different times and places very different mythological efflorescences have been thrown off for the service of the populace; but, underlying each popular religion, the religious knowledge of the initiated minority has been identical. Of course, the modern Western conception of what is right in such matters will be outraged by the mere idea of a religion which is kept as the property of the few, while a "false religion," as modern phraseology would put it is served out to the common people. However, before this feeling is permitted to land us in too uncompromising disapproval of the ancient hiders of the truth, it may be well to determine how far it is due to any intelligent conviction that the common herd would be benefited by teaching, which must be in its nature too refined and subtle for popular comprehension, and how far the feeling referred to, may be due to an acquired habit of looking on religion as something which it is important to profess, irrespective of understanding it. No doubt, assuming that a man's eternal welfare depends upon his declaration, irrespective of comprehension, of the right faith, among all the faiths he might have picked out from the lucky bag of birth and destiny—then it would be the sovereign duty of persons conscious of possessing such a faith to proclaim it from the housetops. But, on the other hypothesis, that it cannot profit any man to mutter a formula of words without attaching sense to it, and that crude intelligences can only be approached by crude sketches of religious ideas, there is more to be advanced on behalf of the ancient policy of reserve than seems at first sight obvious. Certainly the relations of the populace and the initiates, look susceptible of modification in the European world of the present day. The populace, in the sense of the public at large, including the finest intellects of the age, are at least as well able as those of any special class to comprehend metaphysical ideas. These finer intellects dominate public thought, so that no great ideas can triumph among the nations of Europe without their aid, while their aid can only be secured in the open market of intellectual competition. Thus it ensues that the bare notion of an esoteric science superior to that offered in public to the scientific world, strikes the modern Western mind as an absurdity. With which very natural feeling it is only necessary at present here to fight, so far as to ask people not to be illogical in its application; that is to say, not to assume that because it would never occur to a modern European coming into possession of a new truth to make a secret of it, and disclose it only to a fraternity under pledges of reserve, therefore such an idea could never have occurred to an Egyptian priest or an intellectual giant of the civilization which overspread India, according to some not unreasonable hypotheses, before Egypt began to be a seat of learning and art. The secret society system was as natural, indeed, to the ancient man of science, as the public system is in our own country and time. Nor is the difference one of time and fashion merely. It hinges on to the great difference that is to be discerned in the essence of the pursuits in which learned men engage now, as compared with those they were concerned with in former ages. We have belonged to the material progress epoch, and the watchword of material progress has always been publicity. The initiates of ancient psychology belonged to the spiritual age, and the watchword of subjective development has always been secrecy. Whether in both cases the watchword is dictated by necessities of the situation is a question on which discussion might be possible; but, at all events, these reflections are enough to show that it would be unwise to dogmatize too confidently on the character of the philosophy and the philosophers who could be content to hoard their wisdom and supply the crowd with a religion adapted rather to the understanding of its recipients than to those eternal verities.

It is impossible now to form a conjecture as to the date or time at which occult philosophy began to take the shape in which we find it now. But though it may be reasonably guessed that, the last two or three thousand years have not passed over the devoted initiates who have held and transmitted it during that time, without their having contributed something towards its development, the proficiency of initiates belonging to the earliest periods with which history deals, appears to have been already so far advanced, and so nearly as wonderful as the proficiency of initiates in the present day, that we must assign a very great antiquity to the earliest beginnings of occult knowledge on this earth. Indeed the question cannot be raised without bringing us in contact with considerations that hint at absolutely startling conclusions in this respect.

But, apart from specific archaeological speculations, it has been pointed out that "a philosophy so profound, a moral code so ennobling, and practical results so conclusive and so uniformly demonstrable, are not the growth of a generation, or even a single epoch. Fact must have been piled upon fact, deduction upon deduction, science have begotten science, and myriads of the brightest human intellects have reflected upon the laws of Nature, before this ancient doctrine had taken concrete shape. The proofs of this identity of fundamental doctrine in the old religions are found in the prevalence of a system of initiation; in the secret sacerdotal castes, who had the guardianship of mystical words of power, and a public display of a phenomenal control over natural forces indicating association with preter-human beings. Every approach to the mysteries of all these nations, was guarded with the same jealous care, and in all the penalty of death was inflicted upon all initiates of any degree who divulged the secrets entrusted to them." The book just quoted shows this to have been the case with the Eleusinian and Bacchic Mysteries among the Chaldean Magi and the Egyptian Hierophants. The Hindu book of Brahminical ceremonies, the "Agrushada Parikshai," contains the same law, which appears also to have been adopted by the Essenes, the Gnostics, and the Theurgic Neo-Platonists. Freemasonry has copied the old formula, though its *raison d'être* has expired here with the expiration from among freemasons of the occult philosophy on which their forms and ceremonies are shaped to a larger extent than they generally conceive. Evidences of the identity spoken of may be traced in the vows, formulas, rites, and doctrines of various ancient faiths, and it is affirmed by those whom I believe qualified to speak with authority as to the fact, "that not only is their memory still preserved in India; but also that the secret association is still alive, and as active as ever."

As I have now, in support of the views just expressed, to make some quotations from Madame Blavatsky's great book, "Isis Unveiled," it is necessary to give certain explanations concerning the genesis of that work, for which the reader who has followed my narrative of occult experiences through the preceding pages, will be better prepared than he would have been previously. I have shown how, throughout the most ordinary incidents of her daily life, Madame Blavatsky is constantly in communication, by means of the system of psychological telegraphy that the initiates employ, with her superior "Brothers" in occultism. This state of the facts once realised, it will be easy to understand that in compiling such a work as "Isis," which embodies a complete explanation of 'all that can be told about occultism to the outer world, she would not be left exclusively to her own resources, The truth which Madame Blavatsky would be the last person in the world to wish disguised, is that the assistance she derived from the Brothers, by occult agency, throughout the composition of her book, was so abundant and continuous that she is not so much the author of "Isis" as one of a group of *collaborateurs*, by whom it was actually produced. I am given to understand that she set to work on "Isis" without knowing anything about the magnitude of the task she was undertaking, She began writing to dictation—the passages thus written not now standing first in the completed volumes—in compliance with the desire of her occult friends, and without knowing whether the composition on which she was engaged would turn out an article for a newspaper, or an essay for a magazine, or a work of larger dimensions. But on and on it grew. Before going very far, of course, she came to understand what she was about; and fairly launched on her task, she in turn contributed a good deal from her own natural brain. But the Brothers appear always to have been at work with her, not merely dictating through her brain as at first, but sometimes employing those methods of "precipitation" of which I have myself been favoured with some examples, and by means of which quantities of actual manuscript in other handwritings than her own were produced while she slept. In the morning she would sometimes get up and find as much as thirty slips added to the manuscript she had left on her table overnight. The book "Isis" is in fact as great a "phenomenon"—apart from the nature of its contents—as any of those I have described.

The faults of the book, obvious to the general reader, will be thus explained, as well as the extraordinary value it possesses for those who may be anxious to explore as far as possible the mysteries of occultism. The deific powers which the Brothers enjoy cannot protect a literary work which is the joint production of several—even among their minds, from the confusion of arrangement to which such a mode of composition inevitably gives rise. And besides confusion of arrangement, the book exhibits a heterogeneous variety of different styles, which mars its dignity as a literary work, and must prove both irritating and puzzling to the ordinary reader. But for those who possess the key to this irregularity of form, it is an advantage rather than otherwise. It will enable an acute reader to account for some minor incongruities of statement occurring in different parts of the book. Beyond this it will enable him to recognise the voice, as it were, of the different authors as they take up the parable in turn.

The book was written—as regards its physical production—at New York, where Madame Blavatsky was utterly unprovided with books of reference. It teems, however, with references to books of all sorts, including many of a very unusual character, and with quotations the exactitude of which may easily be verified at the great European libraries, as footnotes supply the number of the pages, from which the passages taken are quoted.

I may now go on to collect some passages from "Isis," the object of which is to show the unity of the esoteric philosophy underlying various ancient religions, and the peculiar value which attaches for students of that philosophy, to pure Buddhism, a system which, of all those presented to the world, appears to supply us with occult philosophy in its least adulterated shape. Of course, the reader will guard himself from running away with the idea that Buddhism, as explained by writers who are not occultists, can be accepted as an embodiment of their views. For example, one of the leading ideas of Buddhism, as interpreted by Western scholars, is that "Nirvana" amounts to annihilation. It is possible that Western scholars may be right in saying that the explanation of "Nirvana" supplied by exoteric Buddhism leads to this conclusion; but that, at all events, is not the occult doctrine.

"Nirvana," it is stated in "Isis," "means the certitude of personal immortality in *spirit*, not in *soul*, which, as a finite emanation, must certainly disintegrate its particles, a compound of human sensations, passions, and yearning for some objective kind of existence, before the immortal spirit of the Ego is quite freed, and henceforth secure against transmigration in any form. And how can man reach that state so long as the 'Upadana' that state of longing for life, more life, does not disappear from the sentient being, from the Ahancara clothed, however, in a sublimated body? It is the 'Upadana", or the intense desire that produces will, and it is will which develops force, and the latter generates matter, or an object having form. Thus the disembodied Ego, through this sole undying desire in him, unconsciously furnishes the conditions of his successive self-procreations in various forms, which depend on his mental, state, and 'Karma', the good or bad deeds of his preceding existence, commonly called 'merit' and 'demerit.'" There is a world of suggestive metaphysical thought in this passage, which will serve at once to justify the view propounded just now as regards the reach of Buddhistic philosophy as viewed from the occult standpoint.

The misunderstanding about the meaning of "Nirvana" is so general in the West, that before going on with explanations of the philosophy which this same misunderstanding has improperly discredited, it will be well to consider the following elucidation also:—

"Annihilation means with the Buddhistical philosophy only a dispersion of matter, in whatever form or semblance of form it may be; for every thing that bears a shape was created, and thus must sooner or later perish, *i.e.*, change that shape; therefore, as something temporary, though seeming to be permanent, it is but an illusion, 'Maya'; for as eternity has neither beginning nor end, the more or less prolonged duration of some particular form passes, as it were, like an instantaneous flash of lightning. Before we have the time to realise that we have seen it, it has gone and passed away forever; hence even our astral bodies, pure ether; are but illusions of matter so long as they retain their terrestrial outline. The latter changes, says the Buddhist, according to the merits or demerit of the person during his lifetime, and this is metempsychosis. When the spiritual entity breaks loose for ever from every particle of matter, then only it enters upon the eternal and unchangeable 'Nirvana'. He exists in spirit, in *nothing*; as a form, a shape, a semblance, he is completely annihilated, and thus will die no more; for spirit alone is no 'Maya' but the only reality in an illusionary universe of ever-passing forms... To accuse Buddhistical philosophy of rejecting a Supreme Being-God, and the soul's immortality—of Atheism, in short—on the ground that 'Nirvana' means annihilation, and 'Svabha vat' is not a person, but nothing, is simply absurd. The En (or Aym) of the Jewish Ensoph also means nihil, or *nothing*, that which is not (*quoad nos*), but no one bas ever ventured to twit the Jews with atheism. In both cases the real meaning of the term *nothing* carries with it the idea that God is *not a thing*, not a concrete or visible being to which a name expressive of *any* object known to us on earth may be applied with propriety."

Again: " 'Nirvana' is the world of *cause* in which all deceptive effects or illusions of our senses disappear. 'Nirvana' is the highest attainable sphere."The secret doctrines of the Magi of the pre-Vedic Buddhists, of the hierophants of the Egyptian Thoth or Hermes, were we find it laid down in "Isis"-identical from the beginning, an identity that applied equally to the secret doctrines of the adepts of whatever age or nationality, including the Chaldean Kabalists and the Jewish *Nazars*. "When we use the word Buddhists, we do not mean to imply by it either the exoteric Buddhism instituted by the followers of Gautama Buddha, or the modern Buddhistic religion, but the secret philosophy of Sakyamuni, which, in its essence, is certainly identical with the ancient wisdom—religion of the sanctuary—the pre-vedic Brahmanisn. The schism of Zoroaster, as it is called, is a direct proof of it: for it was no schism, strictly speaking, but merely a partially public exposition of strictly monotheistic religious truths hitherto taught only in the sanctuaries, and that he had learned from the Brahmans. Zoroaster, the primeval institution of sun-worship, cannot be called the founder of the dualistic system, neither was he the first to teach the unity of God, for he taught but what he had learned himself from the Brahmans, And that Zarathustra, and his followers the Zoroastrians, had been settled in India before they immigrated into Persia, is also proved by Max Muller. 'That the Zoroastrians and their ancestors started from India,' he says. 'during the Vaidic period, can be proved as distinctly as that the inhabitants of Massilia started from Greece........... Many of the gods of the Zoroastrians come out....... as mere reflections and deflections of the gods of the Veda.'

"If, now, we can prove, and we ban do so on the evidence of the 'Kabala,' and the oldest traditions of the wisdom religion, the philosophy of the old sanctuaries, that all these gods, whether of the Zoroastrians or of the *Veda*, are but so many personated occult powers of Nature, the faithful servants of the adepts of secret wisdom—magic— we are on secure ground.

"Thus; whether we say that Kabalism and Gnosticism proceeded from Masdeanism or Zoroastrianism, it is all the same, unless we meant the exoteric worship, which we do not. Likewise, and in this sense we may echo King, the author of the 'Gnostics,' and several other archaeologists, and maintain that both the former proceeded from *Buddhism*, at once the simplest and most satisfying of philosophies, and which resulted in one of the purest religions in the world... But whether among the Essenes or the Neo-Platonists, or again among the innumerable struggling sects born but to die, the same doctrine, identical in substance and spirit, if not always in form, are encountered. By *Buddhism*, therefore, we mean that religion signifying literally the doctrine of wisdom, and which by many ages antedates the metaphysical philosophy of Siddhartha Sakyamuni,"

Modern Christianity has, of course, diverged widely from its own original philosophy, but the identity of this with the original philosophy of all religions is maintained in "Isis" in the course of an interesting argument.

"Luke, who was a physician, is designated in the Syriac texts as *Asaia*, the Essaian or Essene. Josephus and Philo Judreus have sufficiently described this sect to leave no doubt in our mind that the Nazarene Reformer, after having received his education in their dwellings in the desert, and being duly initiated in the mysteries, preferred the free and independent life of a wandering *Nazaria*, and so separated, or *inazarenized*, himself, from them, thus becoming a travelling Therapeute, or Nazaria, a healer... In his discourses and sermons Jesus always spoke in parables, and used metaphors with his audience. This habit was again that of the Essenians and the Nazarenes; the Galileans, who dwelt in cities and villages, were never known to use such allegorical language. Indeed, some of his disciples, being Galileans as well as himself, felt even surprised to find him using with the people such a form of expression. 'Why speakest thou unto them in parables?' they often inquired. 'Because it is given unto you to know the mysteries of the kingdom of Heaven; but to them it is not given,' was the reply, which was that of an initiate. 'Therefore, I speak unto them in parables, because they seeing, see not, and hearing, they hear not, neither do they understand.' Moreover, we find Jesus expressing his thoughts... in sentences which are purely Pythagorean, when, during the Sermon on the Mount, he says, 'Give ye not that which is sacred to the dogs, neither cast ye your pearls before swine; for the swine will tread them under their feet, and the dogs will turn and rend you.' Professor A. Wilder, the editor of Taylor's 'Eleusillian Mysteries,' observes a' like disposition on the part of Jesus and Paul to classify their doctrines as esoteric and exoteric—the mysteries of the Kingdom of God for the apostles, and parables for the multitude'. We speak wisdom, says Paul, 'among them that are *perfect*,' or 'initiated.' In the Eleusinian and other mysteries the participants were always divided in two classes, the *neophytes* and the *perfect*... The narrative of the Apostle Paul in his Second Epistle to the Corinthians, has struck several scholars well versed in 'the descriptions of the mystical rites of the initiation given by some classes as all ending most undoubtedly to the final Epopteia: 'I know a certain man—whether in body or outside of body I know not; God knoweth—who was rapt into Paradise, and heard things ineffable which it is not lawful for a man to repeat.' These words have rarely, so far as we know, been regarded by commentators as an allusion 'to the beatific visions of an initiated seer; but the phraseology is unequivocal'. These things which it is not lawful to repeat, are hinted at in the same words, and the reason assigned for it is the same as that which we find repeatedly expressed by Plato, Proclus, Jamblichus, Herodotus, and other classics. 'We speak wisdom only among them that are perfect,' says Paul; the plain and undeniable translation of the sentence being: 'We speak of the profounder or final esoteric doctrines of the mysteries (which are denominated wisdom), only among them who alone initiated. So in relation to the man who was rapt into Paradise—and who was evidently Paul himself—the Christian word Paradise having replaced that of Elysium."

The final purposes of occult philosophy is to show what Man was, is, and will be. "That which survives as an individuality," says 'Isis,' "after the death of the body is the actual soul, which Plato, in the *Timaeus* and *Gorgias* calls the mortal soul; for, according to the Hermetic doctrine, it throws off the more material particles at every progressive change into a higher sphere. The astral spirit is a faithful duplicate of the body in a physical and spiritual sense. The Divine, the highest immortal spirit, can be neither punished nor rewarded. To maintain such a doctrine would be at the same time absurd and blasphemous; for it is not merely a flame lit at the central and inextinguishable fountain of light, but actually a portion of it and of identical essence. It assures immortality to the individual astral being in proportion to the willingness of the latter to receive it. So long as the double man—*i.e.*, the man of flesh and spirit—keeps within the limits of the law of spiritual continuity; so long as the divine spark lingers in him, however faintly, he is on the road to an immortality in the future state. But those who resign themselves to a materialistic existence, shutting out the divine radiance shed by their spirit, at the beginning of their earthly pilgrimage, and stifling the warning voice of that faithful sentry the conscience, which serves as a focus for the light in the soul—such beings as these, having left behind conscience and spirit, and crossed the boundaries of matter, will, of necessity, have to follow its laws."

Again. "The secret doctrine teaches that man, if he wins immortality, will remain for ever the trinity that he is in life, and will continue so throughout all the spheres. The astral body, which in this life is covered by a gross physical envelope, becomes, when relieved of that covering by the process of corporeal death, in its turn the shell of another and more ethereal body. This begins developing from the moment of death, and becomes perfected when the astral body of the earthly form finally separates from it."

The passages quoted, when read by the light of the explanations I have given, will enable the reader, if so inclined, to take up "Isis" in a comprehending spirit, and find his way to the rich veins of precious metal which are buried in its pages. But neither in "Isis" nor in any other book on occult philosophy which has been or seems likely to be written yet awhile, must anyone hope to obtain a cut-and-dried, straightforward, and perfectly clear account of the mysteries of birth, death, and the future. At first, in pursuing studies of this kind, one is irritated at the difficulty of getting at what the occultists really believe as regards the future state, the nature of the life to come, and its general *mise en scène*. The well known religions have very precise views on these subjects, further rendered practical by the assurance some of them give that qualified persons, commissioned by churches to perform the duty, can shunt departing souls on to the right or the wrong lines, in accordance with consideration received. Theories of that kind have at any rate the merit of simplicity and intelligibility, but they are not, perhaps, satisfactory to the mind as regards their details. After a very little investigation of the matter, the student of occult philosophy will realise that on that path of knowledge he will certainly meet with no conceptions likely to outrage his purest idealisation of God and the life to come. He will soon feel that the scheme of ideas he is exploring is lofty and dignified to the utmost limits that the human understanding can reach. But it will remain vague, and he will seek for explicit statements on this or that point, until by degrees he realises that the absolute truth about the origin and destinies of the human soul may be too subtle and intricate to be possibly expressible in straightforward language. Perfectly clear ideas may be attainable for the purified minds of advanced scholars in occultism, who, by entire devotion of every faculty to the pursuit and prolonged assimilation of such ideas, come at length to understand them with the aid of peculiar intellectual powers specially expanded for the purpose; but it does not at all follow that with the best will in the world such persons must necessarily be able to draw up an occult creed which should bring the whole theory of the universe into the compass of a dozen lines. The study of occultism, even by men of the world, engaged in ordinary pursuits as well, may readily enlarge and purify the understanding, to the extent of arming the mind, so to speak, with tests that will detect absurdity in any erroneous religious hypotheses; but the absolute structure of occult belief is something which, from its nature, can only be built up slowly in the mind of each intellectual architect. And I imagine that a very vivid perception of this on their part explains the reluctance of occultists even to attempt the straight—forward explanation of their doctrines.

They know that really vital plants of knowledge, so to speak, must grow up from the germ in each man's mind, and cannot be transplanted into the strange soil of an untrained understanding in a complete state of mature growth. They are ready enough to supply seed, but every man must grow his own tree of knowledge for himself. As the adept himself is not made, but becomes so,—in a minor degree, the person who merely aspires to comprehend the adept and his views of things must develop such comprehension for himself, by thinking out rudimentary ideas to their legitimate conclusions.

These considerations fit in with, and do something towards elucidating, the reserve of occultism, and they further suggest an explanation of what will at once seem puzzling to a reader of "Isis," who takes it up by the light of the present narrative. If great parts of the book, as I have asserted, are really the work of actual adepts, who know of their own knowledge what is the actual truth about many of the mysteries discussed, why have they not said plainly what they meant, instead of beating about the bush, and suggesting arguments derived from this or that ordinary source, from literary or historical evidence, from abstract speculation concerning the harmonies of Nature? The answer seems to be, firstly, that they could not well write, "We know that so and so is the fact," without being asked, "How do you know?"—and it is manifestly impossible that they could reply to this question without going into details, that it would be "unlawful," as a Biblical writer would say, to disclose, or without proposing to guarantee their testimony by manifestations of powers which it would be obviously impracticable for them to keep always at hand for the satisfaction of each reader of the book in turn. Secondly, I imagine that, in accordance with the invariable principle of trying less to teach than to encourage spontaneous development, they have aimed in "Isis," rather at producing an effect on the reader's mind, than at shooting in a store of previously accumulated facts. They have shown that Theosophy, or Occult Philosophy, is no new candidate for the world's attention, but is really a restatement of principles which have been recognised from the very infancy of mankind. The historic sequence which establishes this view is distinctly traced through the successive evolution's of the philosophical schools, in a manner which it is impossible for me to attempt in a work of these dimensions, and the theory laid down is illustrated with abundant accounts of the experimental demonstrations of occult power ascribed to various thaumaturgists. The authors of "Isis," have expressly refrained from saying more than might conceivably be said by a writer who was not an adept, supposing him to have access to all the literature of the subject and an enlightened comprehension of its meaning.

But once realise the real position of the authors or inspirers of "Isis," and the value of any argument on which you find them launched is enhanced enormously above the level of the relatively commonplace considerations advanced on its behalf. The adepts may not choose to bring forward other than exoteric evidence in favour of any particular thesis they wish to support, but if they wish to support it, that fact alone will be of enormous significance for any reader who, in indirect ways, has reached a comprehension of the authority with which they are entitled to speak.

LATER OCCULT PHENOMENA

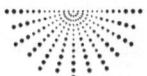

[ADDED TO THE SECOND ENGLISH EDITION.]

I CANNOT let a second edition of this book appear without recording some, at least, of the experiences which have befallen me since its preparation. The most important of these, indeed, are concerned with fragmentary instruction I have been privileged to receive from the Brothers in reference to the great truths of cosmology which their spiritual insight has enabled them to penetrate. But the exposition even of the little, relatively, that I have learned on this head would exact a more elaborate treatise than I can attempt at present.[1] And the purpose of the present volume is to expound the outer facts of the situation rather than to analyse a system of philosophy. This is not entirely inaccessible to exoteric students, apart from what may be regarded as direct revelation from the Brothers. Though almost all existing occult literature is unattractive in its form, and rendered purposely obscure by the use of an elaborate symbology, it does contain a great deal of information that can be distilled from the mass by the application of sufficient patience. Some industrious students of that literature have proved this. Whether the masters of occult philosophy will ultimately consent to the complete exposition in plain language of the state of the facts regarding the spiritual constitution of Man, remains to be seen. Certainly, even if they are still reticent in a way that no ordinary observer can comprehend, they are more disposed to be communicative at this moment than they have been for a long time past.

But the first thing to do is to dissipate as much as possible the dogged disbelief that encrusts the Western mind as to the existence of any abnormal persons who can be regarded as masters of *True* Philosophy —distinguished from all the speculations that have tormented the world —and as to the abnormal nature of their faculties. I have endeavored already to point out plainly, but may as well here emphasise the reason why I dwell upon, the phenomena which exhibit these faculties. Rightly regarded, these are the credentials of the spiritual teaching which their authors supply. Firstly, indeed, *in themselves* abnormal phenomena accomplished by the willpower of living men must be intensely interesting for every one endowed with an honest love of science. They open out new scientific horizons. It is as certain as the sun's next rising that the forward pressure of scientific discovery, advancing slowly as it does in its own grooves, will ultimately, and probably at no very distant date, introduce the ordinary world to some of the superior scientific knowledge already enjoyed by the masters of occultism. Faculties will be acquired by exoteric investigation that will bring the outworks of science a step or two nearer the comprehension of some of the phenomena I have described in the present volume. And meanwhile it seems to me very interesting to get a glimpse beforehand of achievements which we should probably find engaging the eager attention of a future generation, if we really could, as Tennyson suggests—

> *"sleep through terms of mighty wars,*
> *And wake on science grown to more,*
> *On secrets of the brain, the stars,*
> *As wild as aught of fairy lore."*

But even superior to their scientific interest is the importance of the lesson conveyed by occult phenomena, when these distinctly place their authors in a commanding position of intellectual superiority as compared with the world at large. They show most undeniably that these men have gone far ahead of their contemporaries in a comprehension of Nature as exemplified in this world; that they have acquired the power of cognizing events by other means than the material senses; that while their bodies are at one place, their perceptions may be at another, and that they have consequently solved the great problem as to whether the Ego of man is a something distinct from his perishable frame. From all other teachers we can but find out what has been thought probable in reference to the soul or spirit of man; from them we can find out what is the fact; and if that is not a sublime subject of inquiry, surely it would be difficult to say what is. But we cannot read poetry till we have learned the alphabet; and, if the combinations b-a ba, and so on are found to be insufferably trivial and uninteresting, the fastidious person who objects to such foolishness will certainly never be able to read the "Idylls of the King."

So I return from the clouds to my patient record of phenomena, and to the incidents which have confirmed the experiences and conclusions set forth in the previous chapter of this book, since my return to India.

The very first incident which took place was in the nature of a pleasant greeting from my revered friend, Koot Hoomi. I had written to him (per Madame Blavatsky, of course) shortly before leaving London, and had expected to find a letter from him awaiting my arrival at Bombay. But no such letter had been received, as I found when I reached the headquarters of the Theosophical Society, where I had arranged to stay for a few days before going on to my destination up country. I got in late at night, and nothing remarkable happened then. The following morning, after breakfast, I was sitting talking with Madame Blavatsky in the room that had been allotted to me. We were sitting at different sides of a large square table in the middle of the room, and the full daylight was shining. There was no one else in the room. Suddenly, down upon the table before me, but to my right hand, Madame Blavatsky being to my left, there fell a thick letter. It fell "out of nothing", so to speak; it was materialised, or reintegrated in the air before my eyes. It was Koot Hoomi's expected reply—a deeply interesting letter, partly concerned with private matters and replies to questions of mine, and partly with some large, though as yet shadowy, revelations of occult philosophy, the first sketch of this that I had received. Now, of course, I know what some readers will say to this (with a self-satisfied smile)—"wires, springs, concealed apparatus," and so forth; but first all the suggestion would have been grotesquely absurd to anyone who had been present; and secondly, it is unnecessary to argue about objections of this sort all over again *ab initio* every time. There were no more wires and springs about the room I am now referring to, than about the breezy hilltops at Simla, where some of our earlier phenomena took place. I may add, moreover, that some months later an occult note was dropped before a friend of mine, a Bengal civilian, who has become an active member of the Theosophical Society, at a dak bungalow in the north of India; and that later again, at the headquarters of the Theosophical Society at Bombay, a letter was dropped, according to a previous promise, out in the open air in the presence of six or seven witnesses.

For some time the gift of the letter from Koot Hoomi in the way I have described was the only phenomenon accorded to me, and, although my correspondence continued, I was not encouraged to expect any further displays of abnormal power. The higher authorities of the occult world, indeed, had by this time put a very much more stringent prohibition upon such manifestations than had been in operation the previous summer at Simla. The effect of the manifestations then accorded was not considered to have been satisfactory on the whole. A good deal of acrimonious discussion and bad feeling had ensued; and I imagine that this was conceived to outweigh, in its injurious effect on the progress of the Theosophical movement, the good effect of the phenomena on the few persons who appreciated them. When I went up to Simla in August, 1881, therefore, I had no expectation of further events of an unusual nature. Nor have I any stream of anecdotes to relate which will bear comparison with those derived from the experience of the previous year. But nonetheless was the progress of a certain undertaking in which I became concerned—the establishment of a Simla branch of the Theosophical Society—interspersed with little incidents of a phenomenal nature. When this Society was formed, many letters passed between Koot Hoomi and ourselves which were *not* in every case transmitted through Madame Blavatsky. In one case, for example, Mr. Hume, who became president for the first year of the new Society—the Simla Eclectic Theosophical Society, as it was decided it should be called—got a note from Koot Hoomi inside a letter received through the post from a person wholly unconnected with our occult pursuits, who was writing to him in connection with some municipal business. I myself, dressing for the evening, have found an expected letter in my coat-pocket, and on another occasion under my pillow in the morning. On one occasion, having just received a letter by the mail from England which contained matter in which I thought she would be interested, I went up to Madame Blavatsky's writing-room and read it to her. As I read it, a few lines of writing, comment upon what I was reading, were formed on a sheet of blank paper which lay before her. She actually saw the writing form itself, and called to me, pointing to the paper where it lay. There I recognise Koot Hoomi's hand—and his thought, for the comment was to the effect, "Didn't I tell you so?" and referred back to something he had said in a previous letter.

By-the-by, it may be as well to inform the reader that during the whole of the visit to Simla, of which I am now speaking, for several months before it, and until several months later, Colonel Olcott was in Ceylon, where he was engaged in a very successful lecturing tour on behalf of the Theosophical Society, in reference to some of the phenomena which occurred at Simla in 1880, when both he and Madame Blavatsky were present. Ill-natured and incredulous people—when it would be glaringly absurd about some particular phenomenon to say that Madame Blavatsky had done it by trickery of her own—used to be fond of suggesting that the wire-puller must be Colonel Olcott. In some of the newspaper criticisms of the first edition of this book, even, it has been suggested that Colonel Olcott must be the writer of the letters that I innocently ascribe to Koot Hoomi, Madame Blavatsky merely manipulating their presentation. But inasmuch as all through the autumn of 1881, while Colonel Olcott was at Ceylon and I at Simla, the letters continued to come, alternating day by day sometimes with the letters we wrote, my critics, in future, must acknowledge that this hypothesis is played out.

For me myself—as I think it will also be for my appreciative readers—the most interesting fact connected with my Simla experience of 1881 was this:—During the period in question I got into relations with one other of the Brothers, besides Koot Hoomi. It came to pass that in the progress of his own development it was necessary for Koot Hoomi to retire for a period of three months into absolute seclusion, as regards not merely the body—which in the case of an Adept may be secluded in the remotest corner of the earth without that arrangement checking the activity of his "astral" intercourse with mankind—but as regards the whole potent Ego with whom we had dealings. Under these circumstances one of the Brothers with whom Koot Hoomi was especially associated agreed, rather reluctantly at first, to pay attention to the Simla Eclectic Society, and keep us going during Koot Hoomi's absence with a course of instruction in occult philosophy. The change which came over the character of our correspondence when our new master took us in hand was very remarkable. Every letter that emanated from Koot Hoomi had continued to bear the impress of his gently mellifluous style. He would write half a page at any, time rather than run the least risk of letting a brief or careless phrase hurt anybody's feelings. His hand writing, too, was always very legible and regular. Our new master treated us very differently: he declared himself almost unacquainted with our language, and wrote a very rugged hand which it was sometimes difficult to decipher. He did not beat about the bush with us at all. If we wrote out an essay on some occult ideas we had picked up, and sent it to him, asking if it was right, it would sometimes come back with a heavy red line scored through it, and "No" written on the margin. On one occasion one of us had written, "Can you clear my conceptions about so and so?" The annotation found in the margin when the paper was returned was, "How can I clear what you haven't got I" and so on. But with all this we made progress under M—, and by degrees the correspondence, which began on his side with brief notes, scrawled in the roughest manner on bits of coarse Tibetan paper, expanded into considerable letters sometimes. And it must be understood that while his rough and abrupt ways formed an amusing contrast with the tender gentleness of Koot Hoomi, there was nothing in these to impede the growth of our attachment to him as we began to feel ourselves tolerated by him as pupils a little more willingly than at first. Some of my readers, I am sure, will realise what I mean by "attachment" in this case. I use a colourless word deliberately to avoid the parade of feelings which might not be generally understood; but I can assure them that in the course of prolonged relations—even though merely of the epistolary kind—with a personage who, though a man like the rest of us as regards his natural place in creation, is elevated so far above ordinary men as to possess some attributes commonly considered divine, feelings are engendered which are too deep to be lightly or easily described.

It was by M--------- quite recently that a little manifestation of force was given for my gratification, the importance of which turned on the fact that Madame Blavatsky was entirely uninfluential in its production, and eight hundred miles away at the time. For the first three months of my acquaintance with him, M------ had rigidly adhered to the principle he laid down when he agreed to correspond with the Simla Eclectic Society during Koot Hoomi's retirement. He would correspond with us, but would perform no phenomena whatever. This narrative is so much engaged with phenomena that I cannot too constantly remind the reader that these incidents were scattered over a long period of time, and that as a rule nothing is more profoundly distasteful to the great adepts than the production of wonders in the outside world. Ordinary critics of these, when they have been thus exceptionally accorded, will constantly argue, "But why did not the Brothers do so and so differently? then the incident would have been much more convincing." I repeat that the Brothers, in producing abnormal phenomena now and then, are *not* trying to prove their existence to an intelligent jury of Englishmen. They are simply letting their existence become perceptible to persons with a natural gravitation towards spirituality and mysticism. It is not too much to say that all the while they are scrupulously *avoiding* the delivery of direct proof of a nature calculated to satisfy the commonplace mind. For the present, at all events, they prefer that the crass, materialistic Philistines of the sensual, selfish world should continue to cherish the conviction that "the Brothers" are myths. They reveal themselves, therefore, by signs and hints which are only likely to be comprehended by people with some spiritual insight or affinity. True the appearance of this book is permitted by them—no page of it would have been written if a word from Koot Hoomi had indicated disapproval on his part—and the phenomenal occurrences herein recorded are really in many cases absolutely complete and irresistible proofs *for me*, and therefore for anyone who is capable of understanding that I am telling the exact truth. But the Brothers, I imagine, know quite well that, large as the revelation has been, it may safely be passed before the eyes of the public at large just because the herd, whose convictions they do not wish to reach, can be relied upon to reject it. The situation may remind the reader of the *farceur* who undertook to stand on Waterloo Bridge with a hundred real sovereigns on a tray, offering to sell them for a shilling apiece, and who wagered that he would so stand for an hour without getting rid of his stock. He relied on the stupidity of the passers-by, who would think themselves too clever to be taken in. So with this little book. It contains a straightforward statement of absolute truths, which, if people could only believe them, would revolutionise the world; and the statement is fortified by unimpeachable credentials. But the bulk of mankind will be blinded to this condition of things by their own vanity and inability to assimilate super-materialistic ideas, and none will be seriously affected but those who are qualified to benefit by comprehending.

Readers of the latter class will readily appreciate the way the phenomena that I have had to record have thus followed in the track of my own growing convictions, confirming these as they have in turn been inferentially constructed, rather than provoking and enforcing them in the first instance. And this has been emphatically the case with the one or two phenomena that have latterly been accorded by M------. It was in friendship and kindness that these were given, long after all idea of confirming my belief in the Brothers was wholly superfluous and out of date. M------ came indeed to wish that I should have the satisfaction of seeing him (in the astral body of course), and would have arranged for this in Bombay, in January, when I went down there for a day to meet my wife, who was returning from England, had the atmospherical and other conditions just at that period permitted it. But, unfortunately for me, these were not favourable. As M----- wrote in one of several little notes I received from him during that day and the following morning, before my departure from the headquarters of the Theosophical Society, where I was staying, even they, the Brothers, could not "work miracles;" and though to the ordinary spectator there may be but little difference between a miracle and anyone of the phenomena that the Brothers do sometimes accomplish, these latter are really results achieved by the manipulation of natural laws and forces, and are subject to obstacles which are sometimes practically insuperable.

But M------, as it happened, was enabled to show himself to one member of the Simla Eclectic Society, who happened to be at Bombay a day or two before my visit. The figure was clearly visible for a few moments, and the face distinctly recognised by my friend, who had previously seen a portrait of M-------.

Then it passed across the open door of an inner room in which it had appeared, in a direction where there was no exit; and when my friend, who had started forward in its pursuit, entered the inner room, it was no longer to be seen. On two or three other occasions previously, M----- had made his astral figure visible to other persons about the headquarters of the Society, where the constant presence of Madame Blavatsky and one or two other persons of highly sympathetic magnetism, the purity of life of all habitually resident there, and the constant influences poured in by the Brothers themselves, render the production of phenomena immeasurably easier than elsewhere.

And this brings me back to certain incidents which took place recently at my own house at Allahabad, when, as I have already stated, Madame Blavatsky herself was eight hundred miles off, at Bombay. Colonel Olcott, then on his way to Calcutta, was staying with us for a day or two in passing. He was accompanied by a young native mystic, ardently aspiring to be accepted by the Brothers as a *chela*, or pupil, and the magnetism thus brought to the house established conditions which for a short time rendered some manifestations possible. Returning home one evening shortly before dinner, I found two or three telegrams awaiting me, enclosed in the usual way, in envelopes securely fastened before being sent out from the telegraph office. The messages were all from ordinary people, on commonplace business; but inside one of the envelopes I found a little folded note from M-----. The mere fact that it had been thus transfused by occult methods inside the closed envelope was a phenomenon in itself, of course (like many of the same kind that I have described before); but I need not dwell on this point, as the feat that had been performed, and of which the note gave me information, was even more obviously wonderful. The note made me search in my writing-room for a fragment of a plaster bas-relief that M----- had just transported instantaneously from Bombay. Instinct took me at once to the place where I felt that it was most likely I should find the thing which had been brought—the drawer of my writing-table, exclusively devoted to occult correspondence; and there, accordingly, I found a broken corner from a plaster slab, with M——'s signature marked upon it. I telegraphed at once to Bombay, to ask whether anything special had just happened, and next day received back word that M----- had smashed a certain plaster portrait, and had carried off a piece. In due course of time I received a minute statement from Bombay, attested by the signatures of seven persons in all, which was, as regards all essential points, as follows:—

"At about seven in the evening the following persons" (five are enumerated, including Madame Blavatsky) "were seated at the dining-table, at tea, in Madame Blavatsky's veranda opposite the door in the red screen separating her first writing-room from the long veranda. The two halves of the writing-room were wide open, and the dining-table, being about two feet from the door, we could all see plainly everything in the room. About five or seven minutes after, Madame Blavatsky gave a start. We all began to watch. She then looked all round her, and said, 'What is he going to do?' and repeated the same twice or thrice without looking at or referring to any of us. We all suddenly heard a knock—a loud noise, as of something falling and breaking—behind the door of Madame Blavatsky's writing-room, when there was not a soul there at the time. A still louder noise was heard, and we all rushed in. The room was empty and silent; but just behind the red cotton door, where we had heard the noise, we found fallen on the ground a Paris plaster mould, representing a portrait, broken into several pieces. After carefully picking the pieces up to the smallest fragments, and examining it, we found the nail, on which the mould had hung for nearly eighteen months, strong as ever in the wall. The iron wire loop of the portrait was perfectly intact, and not even bent. We spread the pieces on the table, and tried to arrange them, thinking they could be glued, as Madame Blavatsky seemed very much annoyed, as the mould was the work of one of her friends in New York. We found that one piece, nearly square and of about two inches, in the right corner of the mould, was wanting. We went into the room and searched for it, but could not find it. Shortly afterwards, Madame Blavatsky suddenly arose and went into her room, shutting the door after her. In a minute she called Mr. ------in, and showed to him a small piece of paper. We all saw and read it afterwards. It was in the same handwriting in which some of us have received previous communications, and the same familiar initials. It told us that the missing piece was taken by the Brother whom Mr. Sinnett calls, the

Illustrious,[12] To Allahabad, and that she should collect and carefully preserve the remaining pieces." The statement goes after this into some further details, which are unimportant as regards the general reader, and is signed by the four native friends who were with Madame Blavatsky at the time the plaster portrait was broken. A postscript, signed by three other persons, adds that these three came in shortly after the actual breakage, and found the rest of the party trying to arrange the fragments on the table.

It will be understood, of course, but I may s well explicitly state, that the evening to which the above narrative relates was the same on which I found Mr. ——'s note inside my telegram at Allahabad, and the missing piece of the cast in my drawer; and no appreciable time appears to have elapsed between the breakage of the cast at Bombay and the delivery of the piece at Allahabad, for though I did not note the exact minute at which I found the fragment—and, indeed, it may have been already in my drawer for some little time before I came home—the time was certainly between seven and eight, probably about half-past seven or a quarter to eight. And there is nearly half an hour's difference of longitude between Bombay and Allahabad, so that seven at Bombay would be nearly half-past at Allahabad. Evidently, therefore, the plaster fragment, weighing two or three ounces, was really brought from Bombay to Allahabad, to all intents and purposes, instantaneously. That it was veritably the actual piece missing from the cast broken at Bombay was proved a few days later, for all the remaining pieces at Bombay were carefully packed up and sent to me, and the fractured edges of my fragment fitted exactly into those of the defective corner, so that I was enabled to arrange the pieces all together again and complete the cast.

The shrewd reader—of the class of persons who would never have been "taken in" by the man who sold sovereigns on Waterloo Bridge—will laugh at the whole story. A lump of plaster of Paris sent a distance of eight hundred miles across India in the wink of an eye by the willpower of somebody Heaven knows where at the time—probably in Tibet! The shrewd person could not manage the feat himself, so he is convinced that nobody else could, and that the event never occurred. Rather believe that the seven witnesses at Bombay and the present writer are telling a pack of lies than that there can be anyone living in the world who knows secrets of Nature, and can employ forces 'of Nature that shrewd persons of the *Times*-reading, "Jolly Bank-holiday, three-penny 'bus young man" type know nothing about. Some friends of mine, criticising the first edition of this book, have found fault with me for not adopting a more respectful and conciliatory tone towards scientific scepticism when confronting the world with allegations of the kind these pages contain. But I fail to see any motive for hypocrisy in the matter. A great number of intelligent people in these days are shaking themselves free at once from the fetters of materialism forged by modern science and the entangled superstition of ecclesiastics, resolved that the Church herself, with all her mummeries, shall fail to make them irreligious; that science itself, with all its conceit, shall not blind them to the possibilities of Nature. These are the people who will understand my narrative and the sublimity of the revelations it embodies. But all people who have been either thoroughly enslaved by dogma, or thoroughly materialised by modern science, have finally lost some faculties, and will be unable to apprehend facts that do not fit in with their preconceived ideas. They will mistake their own intellectual deficiencies for inherent impossibility of occurrence on the part of the fact described; they will be very rude in thought and speech towards persons of superior intuition, who do find themselves able to believe and, in a certain sense, to understand; and it seems to me that the time has come for letting the commonplace scoffers realise plainly that in the estimation of their more enlightened contemporaries they do indeed seem a Beotian herd, in which the better educated and the lesser educated—the orthodox savant and the city clerk—differ merely in degree and not in kind.

The morning after the occurrence of the incident just detailed, B---- R-----, the young native aspirant for *chelaship*, who had accompanied Colonel Olcott, and was staying at my house, gave me a note from Koot Hoomi, which he found under his pillow in the morning. One which I had written to Koot Hoomi, and had given to B----- R----- the previous day, had been taken, he told me, at night, before he slept. The note from Koot Hoomi was a short one, in the course of which he said, "To force phenomena in the presence of difficulties magnetic or other is forbidden as strictly as for a bank cashier to disburse money which is only entrusted to him. Even to do this much for you so far from the headquarters would be impossible but for the magnetisms O---- and B----- R------,—have brought with them—and I could do no more." Not fully realising the force of the final words in this passage, and more struck by a previous passage, in which Koot Hoomi wrote—" It is easy for us to give phenomenal proofs when we have necessary conditions"—I wrote next day, suggesting one or two things which I thought might be done to take additional advantage of the conditions presented by the introduction into my house of available magnetism different from that of Madame Blavatsky, who had been so much, however

absurdly, suspected of imposing on me. I gave this note to B---- R----
on the evening of the 13th of March—the plaster fragment incident
had taken place on the 11th—and on the morning of the 14th I
received a few words from Koot Hoomi, simply saying that what I
proposed was impossible, and that he would write more fully through
Bombay. When in due time I so heard from him, I learned that the
limited facilities of the moment had been exhausted, and that my
suggestions could not be complied with; but the importance of the
explanations I have just been giving turns on the fact that I did, after
all, exchange letters with Koot Hoomi at an interval of a few hours, at
a time when Madame Blavatsky was at the other side of India.

The account I have just been giving of the instantaneous transmission
of the plaster of Paris fragment from Bombay to Allahabad forms a
fitting prelude to a remarkable series of incidents I have next to record.
The story now to be told has already been made public in India, having
been fully related in "Psychic Notes,"[3] a periodical temporarily brought
out at Calcutta, with the object especially of recording incidents
connected with the spiritualistic mediumship of Mr. Eglinton, who
stayed for some months at Calcutta during the past cold season. The
incident was hardly addressed to the outside world; rather to spiritualists, who while infinitely closer to a comprehension of occultism than
people still wrapped in the darkness of orthodox incredulity, about all
super-material phenomena, are nevertheless to a large extent inclined
to put a purely spiritualistic explanation on *all* such phenomena. In this
way it had come to pass that many spiritualists in India were inclined to
suppose that we who believed in the Brothers were in some way misled
by extraordinary mediumship on the part of Madame Blavatsky. And
at first the "spirit guides" who spoke through Mr. Eglinton confirmed
this view. But a very remarkable change came over their utterances at
last. Shortly before Mr. Eglinton's departure from Calcutta, they
declared their full knowledge of the Brotherhood, naming the "Illustrious" by that designation, and declaring that they had been appointed
to work in concert with the Brothers thenceforth. On this aspect of
affairs, Mr. Eglinton left India in the steamship *Vega*, sailing from
Calcutta, I believe, on the 16th of March. A few days later, on the
morning of the 24th, at AIahabad, I received a letter from Koot
Hoomi, in which he told me that he was going to visit Mr. Eglinton on
board the *Vega* at sea, convince him thoroughly as to the existence of
the Brothers, and if successful in doing this notify the fact immediately
to certain friends of Mr. Eglinton's at Calcutta. The letter had been
written a day or two before, and the night between the 21st and 22nd
was mentioned as the period when the astral visit would be paid. Now

the full explanation of all the circumstances under which this startling programme was carried out will take some little time, but the narrative will be the more easily followed if I first describe the outline of what took place in a few words. 'The promised visit was *actually paid*, and not only that but a letter written by Mr. Eglinton at sea on the 24th describing it—and giving in his adhesion to a belief in the Brothers fully and completely—was transported instantaneously that same evening to Bombay, where it was dropped "out of nothing" like the first letter I received on my return to India before several witnesses; by them identified and tied up with cards written on by them at the time; then taken away again and a few moments later dropped down, cards from Bombay and all, among Mr. Eglinton's friends at *Calcutta* who had been told beforehand to expect a communication from the Brothers at that time. All the incidents of this series are authenticated by witnesses and documents, and there is no rational escape, for any one who looks into the evidence, from the necessity of admitting that the various phenomena as I have just described them have actually been accomplished, "impossible" as ordinary science will declare them.

For the details of the various incidents of the series, I may refer the reader to the account published in *Psychic Notes* of March 30, by Mrs. Gordon, wife of Colonel W. Gordon, of Calcutta, and authenticated with her signature.

Colonel Olcott, Mrs. Gordon explains in the earlier part of her statement, which for brevity's sake I condense, had just arrived at Calcutta on a visit to Colonel Gordon and herself. A letter had come from Madame Blavatsky—

> "dated Bombay the 19th, telling us that something was going to be done, and expressing the earnest hope that she would not be required to assist, as she had had enough abuse about phenomena. Before this letter was brought by the post peon, Colonel Olcott had told me that he had had an intimation in the night from his Chohan (teacher) that K. H.[4] Had been to the *Vega* and seen Eglinton. This was at about eight o'clock on Thursday morning, the 23rd. A few hours later a telegram, dated at Bombay, 22nd day, 21 hours 9 minutes, that is, say 9 minutes past 9 P.M. on Wednesday evening, came to me from Madame Blavatsky, to this effect: 'K. H. just gone to *Vega*.' This telegram came as a 'delayed' message, and was I to me from Calcutta, which accounts for its not reaching me until midday on Thursday. It corroborated, as will be seen, the message of the previous night to Colonel Olcott. We then felt hopeful of getting the letter by occult

means from Mr. Eglinton. A telegram later on Thursday asked us to fix a "time for a sitting, so we named 9 o'clock Madras time, on Friday, 24th. At this hour we three—Colonel Olcott, Colonel Gordon, and myself—sat in the room which had been occupied by Mr. Eglinton.. We had a good light, and sat with our chairs placed to form a triangle, of which the apex was to the north. In a few minutes Colonel Olcott saw outside the open window the two 'Brothers' whose names are best known to us, and told us so; he saw them pass to another window, the glass doors of which were closed. He saw one of them point his hand towards the air over my head, and I felt something at the same moment fall straight down from above on to my shoulder, and saw it fall at my feet in the direction towards the two gentlemen. I knew it would be the letter, but for the moment I was so anxious to see the 'Brothers' that I did not pick up what had fallen. Colonel Gordon and Colonel Olcott both saw and heard the letter fall. Colonel Olcott had turned his head from the window for a moment to see what the I Brother' was pointing at, and so noticed the letter falling from a point about two feet from the ceiling. When he looked again the two 'Brothers' had vanished.

"There is no veranda outside, and the window is several feet from the ground.

"I now turned and picked up what had fallen on me, and found a letter in Mr. Eglinton's handwriting, dated on the *Vega* the 24th; a message from Madame Blavatsky, dated at Bombay the 24th, written on the backs of three of her visiting cards; also a larger card, such as Mr. Eglinton had a packet of, and used at his *séances*. On this latter card was the, to us, well-known handwriting of K. H., and a few words in the handwriting of the other 'Brother,' who was with him outside our window, and who is Colonel Olcott's chief. All these cards and the letter were threaded together with a piece of blue sewing silk. We opened the letter carefully, by slitting up one side, as we saw that some one had made on the flap in pencil three Latin crosses, and so we kept them intact for identification. The letter is as follows:—

"'S. S. *Vega*, Friday, 24th March, 1882.",

My DEAR MRS. GORDON,

—At last your hour of triumph has come! After the many battles we have had at the breakfast-table regarding K. H.'s existence, and my stubborn scepticism as to the wonderful powers possessed by the

"Brothers," I have been forced to a *complete belief* in their being living distinct persons, and just in proportion to my scepticism will be my *firm unalterable opinion* respecting them. I am not allowed to tell you all I know, but K. H. *appeared* to me in person two days ago, and what he told me dumfounded me. Perhaps Madame B. will have already communicated the fact of K. H.'s appearance to you. The "Illustrious" is uncertain whether this can be taken to Madame or not, but he will try, notwithstanding the many difficulties in the way. If he does not I shall post it when I arrive at port. I shall read this to Mrs. B---- and ask her to mark the envelope; but *whatever happens*, you are requested by K. H. to keep this letter a profound secret until you hear from him though Madame. A storm of opposition is certain to be raised, and she has had so much to bear that it is hard she should have more.' Then follow some remarks about his health and the trouble which is taking him home, and the letter ends.

"In her note on the three visiting cards Madame Blavatsky says: —'Headquarters, March 24th. These cards and contents to certify to my doubters that the attached letter addressed to Mrs. Gordon by Mr. Eglinton was just brought to me from the *Vega*, with another letter from himself to me, which I keep. K. H. tells me he saw Mr. Eglinton and had a talk with him, long and convincing enough to make him a believer in the "Brothers," as actual living beings, for the rest of his natural life. Mr. Eglinton writes to me: "The letter which I enclose is going to be taken to Mrs. G. through your influence. You will receive it wherever you are, and will forward it to her in ordinary course. You will learn with satisfaction of my complete conversion to a belief in the "Brothers", and I have no doubt K. H. has already told you how he appeared to me two nights ago," etc., etc.. K. H. *told me all*. He does not, however, want me to forward the letter in "ordinary course", as it would defeat the object, but commands me to write this and send it off without delay, so that it would reach you all at Howrah tonight, the 24th. I do so...

H. P. Blavatsky.'

"The handwriting on these cards and signature are perfectly well known to us. That on the larger card (from Mr. Eglinton's packet) attached was easily recognised as coming from Koot Hoomi . Colonel Gordon and I know his writing as well as our own; it is so distinctly different from any other I have ever seen, that among thousands I could select it. He says, William Eglinton thought the manifestation could only be produced through H. P. B. as a "medium", and that the power would become exhausted at Bombay. We decided otherwise. Let this be a proof to all that the spirit of *living man* has as much potentiality in it (and often more) as a disembodied *soul*. He was anxious to *test her*, he often doubted; two nights ago he had the required proof and will doubt no more. But he is a good young man, bright, honest, and true as gold when once convinced...

"This card was taken from his stock today. Let it be an additional proof of his wonderful mediumship...

K. H.'

"This is written in blue ink, and across it is written in red ink a few words from the other 'Brother' (Colonel Olcott's Chohan or chief). This interesting and wonderful phenomenon is not published with the idea that anyone who is unacquainted with the phenomena of spiritualism will accept it. But I write for the millions of spiritualists, and also that a record may be made of such an interesting experiment. Who knows but that it may pass on to a generation which will be enlightened enough to accept such wonders?"

A postscript adds that since the above statement was written, a paper had been received from Bombay, signed by seven witnesses who saw the letter arrive there from the *Vega*.

As I began by saying, this phenomenon was addressed more to spiritualists than to the outer world, because its great value for the experienced observer of phenomena turns on the utterly unmediumistic character of the events. Apart from the testimony of Mr. Eglinton's own letter to the effect that he, an experienced medium, was quite convinced that the interview he had with his occult visitant was not an interview with such "spirits" as he had been used to, we have the three-cornered character of the incident to detach it altogether from mediumship either on his part or on that of Madame Blavatsky.

Certainly there have been cases in which under the influence or mediumship the agencies of the ordinary spiritual *séance* have transported letters half across the globe. A conclusively authenticated case in which an unfinished letter was thus brought from London to Calcutta will have attracted the attention of all persons who have their understanding awakened to the importance of these matters, and who read what is currently published about them, quite recently. But every spiritualist will recognise that the transport of a letter from a ship at sea to

Bombay, and then from Bombay to Calcutta, with a definite object in view, and in accordance with a prearranged and pre-announced plan, is something quite outside the experience of mediumship.

Will the effort made and the expenditure of force, whatever may have been required to accomplish the wonderful feat thus recorded, be repaid by proportionately satisfactory effects on the spiritualistic world? There has been a great deal written lately in England about the antagonism between spiritualism and theosophy, and an impression has arisen in some way that the two *cultes* are incompatible. Now, the phenomena and the experiences of spiritualism are facts, and nothing can be incompatible with facts. But theosophy brings on the scene new interpretations of those facts, it is true, and sometimes these prove very unwelcome to spiritualists long habituated to their own interpretation. Hence, such spiritualists are now and then disposed to resist the new teaching altogether, and hold out against a belief that there can be anywhere in existence men entitled to advance it. This is consequently the important question to settle before we advance into the region of metaphysical subtleties. Let spiritualists once realise that the Brothers do exist, and what sort of people they are, and a great step will have been accomplished. Not all at once is it to be expected that the spiritual world will consent to revise its conclusions by occult doctrines. It is only by prolonged intercourse with the Brothers that a conviction grows up in the mind that as regards spiritual science they *cannot* be in error. At first, let spiritualists think them in error if they please; but at all events it will be unworthy of their elevated position above the Beotian herd if they deny the evidence of phenomenal facts; if they hold towards occultism the attitude which the crass sceptic of the mere Lankester type occupies towards spiritualism itself. So I cannot but hope that the coruscation of phenomena connected with the origin and adventures of the letter written on board the *Vega* may have flashed out of the darkness to some good purpose, showing the spiritualistic world quite plainly that the great Brother to whom this work is dedicated is, at all events, a living man, with faculties and powers of that entirely abnormal kind which spiritualists have hitherto conceived to inhere merely in beings belonging to a superior scheme of existence.

For my part, I am glad to say that I not only know him to be a living man by reason of all the circumstances detailed in this volume, but I am now enabled to realise his features and appearance by means of two portraits, which have been conceded to me under very remarkable conditions. It was long a wish of mine to possess a portrait of my revered friend; and some time ago he half promised that some time or other he would give me one. Now, in asking an adept for his portrait, the object desired is not a photograph, but a picture produced by a certain occult process which I have not yet had occasion to describe, but with which I had long been familiar by hearsay. I had heard, for example, from Colonel Olcott, of one of the circumstances under which his own original convictions about the realities of occult power were formed many years ago in New York, before he had actually entered on "the path." Madame Blavatsky on that occasion had told him to bring her a piece of paper which he would be certainly able to identify, in order that she might get a portrait precipitated upon it. We cannot, of course, by the light of ordinary knowledge form any conjecture about the details of the process employed; but just as an adept can, as I have had so many proofs, precipitate writing in closed envelopes, and on the pages of uncut pamphlets, so he can precipitate color in such a way as to form a picture. In the case of which Colonel Olcott told me he took home a piece of note-paper from a club in New York —a piece bearing a club stamp—and gave this to Madame Blavatsky. She put it between the sheets of blotting-paper on her writing-table, rubbed her hand over the outside of the pad, and then in a few moments the marked paper was given back to him with a complete picture upon it representing an Indian fakir in a state of *samadhi*. And the artistic execution of this drawing was conceived by artists to whom Colonel Olcott afterwards showed it to be so good that they compared it to the works of old masters whom they specially adored and affirmed that as an artistic curiosity it was unique and priceless. Now in aspiring to have a portrait of Koot Hoomi, of course I was wishing for a precipitated picture, and it would seem that just before a recent visit Madame Blavatsky paid to Allahabad, something must have been said to her about a possibility that this wish of mine might be gratified. For the day she came she asked me to give her a piece of thick white paper and mark it. This she would leave in her scrapbook, and there was reason to hope that a certain highly advanced *chela*, or pupil, of Koot Hoomi's, not a full adept himself as yet, but far on the road to that condition, would do what was necessary to produce the portrait.

Nothing happened that day nor that night. The scrapbook remained lying on a table in the drawing-room, and was occasionally inspected. The following morning it was looked into by my wife, and my sheet of paper was found to be still blank. Still the scrapbook lay in full view on the drawing-room table. At half-past eleven we went to breakfast; the dining-room, as is often the case in Indian bungalows, only being separated from the drawing-room by an archway and curtains, which were drawn aside. While we were at breakfast Madame Blavatsky suddenly showed, by the signs with which all who know her are familiar, that one of her occult friends was near. It was the *chela* to whom I have above referred. She got up, thinking she might be required to go to her room; but the astral visitor, she said, waved her back, and she returned to the table. After breakfast we looked into the scrapbook, and on my marked sheet of paper, which had been seen blank by my wife an hour or two before, was a precipitated profile portrait. The face itself was left white, with only a few touches within the limits of the space it occupied; but the rest of the paper all round it was covered with cloudy blue shading. Slight as the method was by which the result was produced, the outline of the face was perfectly well-defined, and its expression as vividly rendered as would have been possible with a finished picture.

At first Madame Blavatsky was dissatisfied with the sketch. Knowing the original personally, she could appreciate its deficiencies; but though I should have welcomed a more finished portrait, I was sufficiently pleased with the one I had thus received to be reluctant that Madame Blavatsky should try any experiment with it herself with the view of improving it, for fear it would be spoilt. In the course of the conversation, M---- put himself in communication with Madame Blavatsky, and said that he would do a portrait himself on another piece of paper. There was no question in this case of a "test phenomenon"; so after I had procured and given to Madame Blavatsky a (marked) piece of Bristol board, it was put away in the scrapbook, and taken to her room, where, free from the confusing cross magnetisms of the drawing-room, M---- would be better able to operate.

Now it will be understood that neither the producer of the sketch I had received, nor M-----, in the natural state, is an artist. Talking over the whole subject of these occult pictures, I ascertained from Madame Blavatsky that the supremely remarkable results have been obtained by those of the adepts whose occult science as regards this particular process has been superseded to ordinary artistic training. But entirely without this, the adept can produce a result which, for all ordinary critics, looks like the work of an artist, by merely realising very clearly in his imagination the result he wishes to produce, and then precipitating the coloring matter in accordance with that conception.

In the course of about an hour from the time at which she took away the piece of Bristol board—or the time may have been less—we were not watching it, Madame Blavatsky brought it me back with another portrait, again a profile, though more elaborately done. Both portraits were obviously of the same face, and nothing, let me say at once, can exceed the purity and lofty tenderness of its expression. Of course it bears no mark of age. Koot Hoomi, by the mere years of his life, is only a man of what we call middle age; but the adept's physically simple and refined existence leaves no trace of its passage; and while our faces rapidly wear out after forty—strained, withered, and burned up by the passions to which all ordinary lives are more or less exposed —the adept age, for periods of time that I can hardly venture to define, remains apparently the perfection of early maturity. M-----, Madame Blavatsky's special guardian still, as I judge by a portrait of him that I have seen, though I do not yet possess one, in the absolute prime of manhood, has been her occult guardian from the time she was a child; and now she is an old lady. He never looked, she tells me, any different from what he looks now.

I have now brought up to date the record of all external facts connected with the revelations I have been privileged to make. The door leading to occult knowledge is still ajar, and it is still permissible for explorers from the outer world to make good their footing across the threshold. This condition of things is due to exceptional circumstances at present, and may not continue long. Its continuance may largely depend upon the extent to which the world at large manifests an appreciation of the opportunity now offered. Some readers who are interested, but slow to perceive what practical action they can take, may ask what they can do to show appreciation of the opportunity. My reply will be modelled on the famous injunction of Sir Robert Peel: "Register, register, register!" Take the first steps towards making a response to the offer which emanates from the occult world—register, register, register; in other words, join the Theosophical Society—the one and only association which at present is linked by any recognised bond of union with the Brotherhood of Adepts in Tibet. There is a Theosophical Society in London, as there are other branches in Paris and America, as well as in India. If there is as yet but little for these branches to do, that fact does not vitiate their importance. After a voter has registered, there is not much for *him* to do for the moment. The mere growth of branches of the Theosophical Society, as associations of people who realise the sublimity of adeptship, and have been able to feel that the story told in this little book, and more fully, if more obscurely, in many greater volumes of occult learning, is absolutely true —true, not as shadowy religious "truths" or orthodox speculations are held to be true by their votaries, but true as the "London Post-Office Directory" is true; as the Parliamentary reports people read in the morning are true; the mere enrolment of such people in a society under conditions which may enable them sometimes to meet and talk the situation over if they do no more, may actually effect a material result as regards the extent to which the authorities of the occult world will permit the further revelation of the sublime knowledge they possess. Remember, that knowledge is real knowledge of other worlds and other states of existence—not vague conjecture about hell and heaven and purgatory, but precise knowledge of other worlds going on at this moment, the condition and nature of which the adepts can cognize, as we can the condition and nature of a strange town we may visit. These worlds are linked with our own, and our lives with the lives they support; and will the further acquaintance with the few men on earth who are in a position to tell us more about them be superciliously rejected by the advance guard of the civilized world, the educated classes of England? Surely no inconsiderable group will be sufficiently spiritualized to comprehend the value of the present opportunity, and sufficiently practical to follow the advice already quoted, and—register, register, register.

---

1. Subsequently published as Esoteric Buddhism.
2. "My illustrious friend," was the expression I originally used in application to the Brother I have here called M—, and it got shortened afterwards into the pseudonym given in the statement. It is difficult sometimes to know what to call the Brothers, even when one knows their real names. The less these are promiscuously handled the better, for various reasons, among which is the profound annoyance which it gives their real disciples if such names get into frequent and disrespectful use among scoffers. I regret now that Koot Hoomi's name, so ardently venerated by all who have been truly subject to his influence, should ever have been allowed to appear in full in the text of the book.
3. Newton & Co., Calcutta.
4. We had got into the habit at this time of using these initials for the Mahatma's name.

APPENDIX

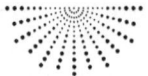

A

LATER acquaintance with the subject has done much to show me that the reserve hitherto maintained by the masters of occult science was inevitable. It is useless to offer any man information which his faculties are not sufficiently expanded to receive. Only a few hundred years after the physical science that has been absorbed by the last two or three generations with avidity would have been unwelcome and despised. Till quite recently the serious contemplation of psychic phenomena would have been resented as a relapse into superstition. No man can investigate causes till he is willing to observe facts, and it was only the other day that a disposition to observe facts lying outside the domain of physical causation would have alienated any prematurely developed enthusiast from the sympathies of all his contemporaries. The light of mere worldly wisdom may thus vindicate the reticence of the few and secluded custodians of the higher knowledge, but with far greater precision is their policy vindicated when with their own help we come at last to comprehend the scientific law of human intellectual development. The progress of the world is not rolling on under the direction of blind chance. Propelled though it is by the collective impulses of individual energy, it advances in a defined path, and the knowledge, the discoveries, the spiritual teaching, which breaks upon the world at each stage of its advancement, is precisely proportioned to the receptivity of mankind at that period of its evolution. The revelation of occult truth going on in the world just now in many ways and under various aspects—though as I most emphatically believe, under none more unequivocally or satisfactorily than in the case of the direct teaching of occult science I am instrumental in bringing to public notice—is the legitimate inheritance of this generation, and the good it may do in the world now could not have been done only a few decades ago. It is useless to try to take a photographic picture upon a non-sensitized plate; it is useless to present the subtle conceptions of spiritual science to minds on which no psychic collodion has previously been deposited. The Esoteric study in which some of us connected with the Theosophical Society have been privileged, during the last two or three years, to engage, has so effectually dispelled the discontent we first felt at the jealousy that had withheld this teaching from the world so long, that we recognise the message we are now commissioned to convey as addressed so far only to the most highly advanced and intuitive minds of our time. We are but beginning to put forward a doctrine which will only be appreciated in its full significance later on.

—June 7, 1884.

B.

It is interesting to observe that, in accordance with predictions made to me when I began to write on these subjects, the dawn of psychic truth has begun to brighten our sky from several directions at once. The psychological telegraphy here referred to was quite unheard of In the world at large in 1880. But for the last year or two the Psychic Research Society in London has been specially engaged on a long series of experiments in what it calls "thought transference," the phenomena of which contain the germs of the adepts' psychic telegraph. If anyone still doubts that thought impressions really can be conveyed from one mind to another, without the aid of speech or any sign or communication whatever having to do with the physical senses, he is unacquainted with the result of scientific enquiry in that direction. The transactions of the society referred to put the broad fact just noted beyond the reach of incredulity that can any longer be regarded as intelligent.

C

It is too late in the day now, when several editions of this book have already passed through the press, to affect any reserve about this name.

But in truth I greatly regret now that I ever permitted it to become public property. All over India the disciples of the Brothers regard their Masters' names with the tenderest possible respect. The free and easy criticism to which this book has naturally been subject since its first appearance has often been associated with more or less disrespectful references to my revered correspondent, and this has given rise to great pain on the part of the regular *chelas* in India, the pupils of occult science; indeed, it is no longer necessary to go to India in search of persons whose sensibilities are liable to be disturbed seriously in the same way. In London a large and earnestly studious branch of the Theosophical Society has been formed, and long contact with the grand conceptions of Esoteric philosophy has developed on the part of its members a sentiment of reverence for the Mahatmas only second in intensity to that of the regular oriental initiates. It would spare all such persons a great deal of indignant distress, if the name I was unfortunately led to print in this work at full length had never been disclosed. To most Western readers the matter may seem very unimportant, but trouble and annoyance which I greatly deplore have ensued from the mistake thus committed. As a matter of fact, I may here observe that the original manuscript of my book, was written from end to end without the use of the name, instead of, which I had placed a mere initial, "H", but a letter I received from India shortly before the publication of the book authorised the use of the name, and I felt at that time that it was absurd to be *plus royaliste que le roi*. So the step came to be taken which cannot now be recalled. The name of the Mahatma here made use of, I may explain, in conclusion of this digression.

D

The necessity of reprinting this work for a fourth edition gives me an opportunity of noticing some discussion that has taken place in the spiritualistic press on the subject of a letter addressed to *Light*, of September 1st, 1883, by Mr. Henry Kiddle, an American spiritualist. The letter was as follows:

To THE EDITOR OF "*LIGHT*."

SIR,

—In a communication that appeared in your issue of July 21st, "'G. W., M.D.," reviewing '"Esoteric Buddhism," says: Regarding this Koot Hoomi, it is a very remarkable and unsatisfactory fact that Mr.

Sinnett, although in correspondence with him for years, has yet never been permitted to see him."I agree with your corespondent entirely; and this is not the only fact that is unsatisfactory to me. On reading Mr. Sinnett's "Occult World," more than a year ago, I was very greatly surprised to find in one of the letters presented by Mr. Sinnett as having been transmitted to him by Koot Hoomi, in the mysterious manner described, a passage taken almost *verbatim* from an address on Spiritualislm by me at Lake Pleasant in August, 1880, and published the same month by the *Banner of Light*. As Mr. Sinnett's book did not appear till a considerable time afterwards (about a year, I think), it is certain that I did not quote, consciously or unconsciously, from its pages. How, then, did it get into Koot Hoomi's mysterious letter?

I sent to Mr. Sinnett a letter through his publishers, enclosing the printed pages of my address, with the part used by Koot Hoomi marked upon it, and asked for an explanation, for I wondered that so great a sage as Koot Hoomi should need to *borrow* anything from so humble a student of spiritual things as myself. As yet I have received no reply; and the query has been suggested to my mind—Is Koot Hoomi a myth? or, if not, is he so great an adept as to have impressed my mind with his thoughts and word while I was preparing my address?If the latter were the case he could not consistently exclaim: '"*Pereant qui ante nos nostra dixerunt.*"

Perhaps Mr. Sinnett may think it scarcely worth while to solve this little problem; but the fact that the existence of the brotherhood has not yet been proved may induce some to raise the question suggested by "G. W., M. D". Is there any such secret order? On this question, which is not intended to imply anything offensive to Mr. Sinnett, that other still more important question may depend. Is Mr. Sinnett's recently published book an exponent of Esoteric Buddhism? It Is, doubtless, a work of great ability, and its statements are worthy of deep thought; but the main question is, are they true, or how can they be verified?' As this cannot he accomplished except by the exercise of abnormal or transcendental faculties, they must be accepted, if at all, upon the *ipse dixit* of the accomplished adept, who has been so kind as to sacrifice his esoteric character or vow, and make Mr. Sinnett his channel of communication with the outer world, thus rendering his sacred knowledge exoteric. Hence, if this publication, with its wonderful doctrine of Shells,"overturning the consolatory conclusions of Spiritualists, is to be accepted, the authority must he established, and the existence of the adept or adepts—indeed, the facts of adeptship—must be proved. The first step in affording this proof has hardly yet, I think, been taken. I trust this book will be very carefully analysed, and the nature of its inculcations exposed, whether they are Esoteric Buddhism or not,

The following are the passages referred to, printed side by side[1]—for the sake of ready reference.

Extract from Mr. Kiddle's discourse, entitled "The Present Outlook of Spiritualism", delivered at Lake Pleasant Camp Meeting on Sunday, August 15, 1880.

"My friends, *ideas* rule the world; and as men's minds receive new ideas, laying aside the old and effete, the world advances. Society rests upon them; mighty revolutions spring from them; institutions crumble before their onward march. It is just as impossible to resist their influx, when the time comes, as to stay the progress of the tide.

And the agency called Spiritualism is bringing a new set of ideas into the world—ideas on the most momentous subjects, touching man's true position in the universe; his origin and destiny; the relation of the mortal to the immortal; of the temporary to the Eternal; of the finite to the Infinite; of man's deathless soul to the material universes in which it now dwells—ideas larger, more general, more comprehensive, recognising more fully the universal reign of law as the expression of the Divine will, unchanging and unchangeable in regard to which there is only an *Eternal Now*, while to mortals time is past or future, as related to their finite existence on this material plane; etc., etc., etc.,

New York, August 11th, 1883

Extract from Koot Hoomi's letter to Mr. Sinnett, in the "Occult World", 3rd Edition, page 102. The first edition was published in June 1881.

Ideas rule the world; and as men's minds receive new ideas, laying aside the old and effete, the world will advance, mighty revolutions will spring from them, creeds and even powers will crumble before their onward march, crushed by their irresistible force. It will be just as impossible to resist their influence when the time comes as to stay the progress of the tide. But all this will come gradually on, before it comes we have a duty set before us; that of sweeping away as much as possible the dross left to us by our pious forefathers. New ideas have to be planted on clean places, for these ideas touch upon the most momentous subjects. It is not physical phenomena, but these universal ideas that we study, as to comprehend the former, we have first to understand the latter. They touch man's true position in the universe in relation to his previous and future births, his origin and ultimate destiny; the relation of the mortal to the immortal, of the temporary to the Eternal, of the finite to the Infinite; ideas larger, grander, more comprehensive, recognising the eternal reign of immutable law, unchanging and unchangeable, in regards to which there is only an ETERNAL NOW; while to uninitiated mortals time is past or future as related to their finite existence on this material speck of dirt, etc., etc., etc.

HENRY KIDDLE.

The appearance of this letter puzzled, without very much disturbing, the equanimity of Theosophical students. If it had been published immediately after the first publication of the "Occult World," its effect might have been more serious, but in the interim the Brothers had by degrees communicated to the public through my agency such a considerable block of philosophical teaching, then already embodied in my second book, "*Esoteric Buddhism*," and scattered through two or three volumes of the *Theosophist*, that appreciative readers had passed beyond the stage of development in which it might have been possible for them to suppose that the principal author of this teaching could at any time have been under any intellectual temptation to borrow thoughts from a spiritualistic lecture. Various hypotheses were framed to account for the mysterious identity between the two passages cited, and people to whom the Theosophic teachings were unacceptable, as overthrowing conceptions to which they were attached, were greatly enchanted to find my revered instructor convicted, as they thought, of a commonplace plagiarism. A couple of months necessarily elapsed before an answer could be obtained from India on the subject, and meanwhile the "Kiddle incident," as it came to be called, was joyfully treated by various correspondents writing in the columns of *Light*, as having dealt a fatal blow at the authority of the Indian Mahatmas as exponents of esoteric truth.

In due course I received a long and instructive explanation of the mystery from Mahatma Koot Hoomi himself; but this letter reached me under the seal of the most absolute confidence. Rigidly adhering to the policy which had all along restrained within narrow limits the communication of their teaching to the world at large, the Brothers remained as anxious as ever to leave everybody full intellectual liberty to disbelieve in them, and reject their revelation if his spiritual intuitions were not of a kind to be readily kindled. In the same way that from the first they had refused me the overwhelming and irresistible proofs of their power, which I had sought for in the beginning as weapons with which I might successfully combat incredulity, they now shrank from interfering with the conclusions of any readers who might be found capable, after the rich assurances of the later teaching, of distrusting the Mahatmas on the strength of a suspicion which was ill founded in reality, plausible though it might seem. Debarred myself, however, from making any public use of the Mahatma's letter, some of the residents and visitors at the Headquarters of the Theosophical Society at Adyar, Madras, came into possession of the true facts of the case, and some communications appeared in the society's magazine which afforded everyone honestly desirous of comprehending the truth of the matter, all necessary information. In the December number of the *Theosophist*, Mr. Subba Row put forward a very cautiously worded article, hinting merely at the actual explanation of the identity of the passages cited by Mr. Kiddle, and concerned chiefly with an elaborate analysis of the "plagiarised" sentences, the object of which was to show that in truth we might have divined for ourselves, if we had been sharp enough in the beginning, that some mistake had been made, and that the Mahatma could not have intended to write the sentences just as they stood. The hint conveyed by Mr. Subba was as follows:—

> "Therefore from a careful perusal of the passage and its contents, any unbiased reader will come to the conclusion that somebody must have greatly blundered over the said passage, and will not be surprised to hear that it was unconsciously altered through the carelessness and ignorance of the *chela* by whose instrumentality it was 'precipitated.' Such alterations, omissions, and mistakes sometimes occur in the process of precipitation; and I now assert I know it for certain, from an inspection of the original precipitation proof, that such was the case with regard to the passage under discussion."

The same *Theosophist* in which this article appeared contained a letter from General Morgan in reply to various spiritualistic attacks on the Theosophical position, and in the course of his remarks he referred to the "Kiddle incident" as follows:—

> "Happily we have been permitted, many of us, to look behind the veil of the parallel passage mystery, and the whole affair is very satisfactorily explained to us; but all that we are permitted to say is

that many a passage was entirely omitted from the letter received by Mr. Sinnett, its precipitation from the original dictation to the *chela*. Would our Great Master but permit us his humble followers to photograph and publish in the *Theosophist* the scraps shown to us, scraps in which whole sentences parenthetical and quotation marks are defaced and obliterated and consequently omitted in the *chela*' clumsy transcription—the public would be treated to a rare sight— something entirely unknown to modern science—namely, an *akasic* impression as good as a photograph of mentally expressed thoughts dictated from a distance."

A month or two after the appearance of these fragmentary hints, I received a note from the Mahatma relieving me of all restrictions previously imposed on the full letter of explanation he had previously sent me. The subject, by that time, however, seemed to have lost its interest for all persons in England whose opinions I valued. Within the London Theosophical Society, now already a large and growing body, the Kiddle incident was looked on as little more than a joke, and the notion that the Mahatma who had inspired the teachings of Esoteric Buddhism, could have "plagiarised" from a spiritualistic lecture, as so absurd on the face of things that no appearances seeming to endorse that conception could have any importance. I did not feel disposed, therefore, to treat the suspicions some critics had entertained, with the respect that would have been involved in any appeal from me to the public to listen to what would have been represented as a defence—and a strangely postponed defence—of the Mahatma.

Now, however, that this new edition of the Occult World II is required, there is an obvious propriety in the course I now take. The new letter from the Mahatma constitutes in itself a correction of the letter from which I quote on pages 101-102, and apart from the interest of the explanation it furnishes in regard to the precipitation process, the thoughts it conveys are in themselves valuable and suggestive.

"The letter in question," writes the Mahatma, referring to the communication I originally received, "was framed by me while on a journey and on horseback. It was dictated mentally in the direction of and precipitated by a young *chela* not yet expert at this branch of psychic chemistry, and who had to transcribe it from the hardly visible imprint. Half of it, therefore, was omitted, and the other half more or less distorted by the 'artist.' When asked by him at the time whether I would look over and correct it, I answered—imprudently, I confess —"Anyhow will do, my boy; it is of no great importance if you skip a few words.'I was physically very tired by a ride of forty-eight hours consecutively, and (physically again) half asleep. Besides this, I had very important business to attend to psychically, and therefore little remained of me to devote to that letter. When I awoke I found it had already been sent on, and as I was not then anticipating its publication, I never gave it from that time a thought. Now I had never evoked spiritual Mr. Riddle's physiognomy, never had heard of his existence, was not aware of his name. Having, owing to our correspondence, and your Simla surroundings and friends, felt interested in the intellectual progress of the Phenomenalists, I had directed my attention, some two months previous, to the great annual camping movement of the American Spiritualists in various directions, among others to Lake or Mount Pleasant. Some of the curious ideas and sentences representing the general hopes and aspirations of the American Spiritualists remained impressed on my memory, and I remembered only these ideas and detached sentences quite apart from the personalities of those who harboured or pronounced them. Hence my entire ignorance of the lecturer whom I have innocently defrauded, as it would appear, and who raises the hue and cry. Yet had I dictated my letter in the form it now appears in print, it would certainly look suspicious, and however far from what is generally called plagiarism, yet in the absence of any inverted commas it would lay a foundation for censure. But I did nothing of the kind, as the original impression now before me clearly shows. And before I proceed any further I must give you some explanation of this mode of precipitation.

The recent experiments of the Psychic Research Society will help you greatly to comprehend the rationale of this mental telegraphy. You have observed in the journal of that body, how thought transference is cumulatively effected. The image of the geometrical or other figure which the active brain has had impressed upon it is gradually imprinted upon the recipient brain of the passive subject, as the series of reproductions illustrated in the cuts show. Two factors are needed to produce a perfect and instantaneous mental telegraphy—close concentration in the operator and complete receptive passivity in the reader subject. Given a disturbance of either condition, and the result is proportionately imperfect. The reader does not see the image as in the telegrapher's brain, but as arising in his own. When the latter's thought wanders, the psychic current becomes broken, the communication disjointed and incoherent. In a case such as mine the *chela* had, as it were, to pick up what he could from the current I was sending him, and, as above remarked, patch the broken bits together as best he might. Do not you see the same thing in ordinary mesmerism—the *maya* impressed upon the subject's imagination by the operator becoming now stronger, now feebler, as the latter keeps the intended illusive image more or less steadily before his own fancy. And how often the clairvoyants reproach the magnetiser for taking their thoughts off the subject under consideration. And the mesmeric healer will always bear you witness that if he permits himself to think of anything but the vital current he is pouring into his patient, he is at once compelled to either establish the current afresh or stop the treatment. So I, in this instance, having at the moment more vividly in my mind the psychic diagnosis of current spiritualistic thought, of which the Lake Pleasant speech was one marked symptom, unwittingly transferred that reminiscence more vividly than my own remarks upon it and deductions therefrom. So to say, the 'despoiled victim's'—Mr. Kiddle's—utterances came out as a high light, and were more sharply photographed (first, in the *chela*'s brain, and thence on the paper before him, a double process, and one far more difficult than thought reading simply), while the rest, my remarks thereupon and arguments—as I now find, are hardly visible and quite blurred on the original scraps before me. Put into a mesmeric subject's hand a sheet of bank paper, tell him it contains a certain chapter of some book that you have read, concentrate your thoughts upon the words, and see how—provided that he has himself not read the chapter, but only takes it from your memory, his reading will reflect your own more or less vivid successive recollections of your author's language. The same as to the precipitation by the *chela* of the transferred thought upon (or rather into) paper. If the mental picture received be feeble, his visible reproduction of it must correspond. And the more so in proportion to the closeness of attention he gives. He might—were he but merely a person of the true mediumistic temperament—be employed by his "Master" as a sort of psychic printing machine (producing lithographed or psychographed impressions of what the operator had in mind; his nerve system the machine, his nerve aura the printing fluid, the colors drawn from that exhaustless storehouse of pigments (as of everything else) the akasa. But the medium and the *chela* are diametrically dissimilar, and the latter acts consciously, except under exceptional circumstances, during development not necessary to dwell upon here.

"Well, as soon as I heard of the change, the commotion among my defenders having reached me across the eternal snows, I ordered an investigation into the original scraps of the impression. At the first glance I saw that it was I the only and most guilty party, the poor boy having done hut that which he was told. Having now restored the characters and the lines omitted and blurred beyond hope of recognition by anyone but their original evolver, to their primitive color and places, I now find my letter reading quite differently, as you will observe. Turning to the 'Occult World', the copy sent by you, to the page cited, I was struck, upon carefully reading it, by the great discrepancy between the sentences, a gap, so to say, of ideas between part 1 and part 2, the plagiarised portion so called. There seems no connection at all between the two; for what has indeed the determination of our chiefs (to prove to a sceptical world that physical phenomena are as reducible to law as anything else) to do with Plato's ideas which 'rule the world,' or 'Practical Brotherhood of Humanity.' I fear that it is your personal friendship alone for the writer that has blinded you to the discrepancy and disconnection of ideas in this abortive precipitation even until now. Otherwise you could not have failed to perceive that something was wrong on that page, that there was a glaring defect in the connection. Moreover, I have to plead guilty to another sin: I have never so much as looked at my letters in print, until the day of the forced investigation. I had read only your own original matter, feeling it a loss of time to go over my hurried bits and scraps of thought. But now I have to ask you to read the passages as they were originally dictated by me, and make the comparison with the 'Occult World' before you...I enclose the copy verbatim from the restored fragments, underlining in red the omitted sentences for easier comparison.

"...Phenomenal elements previously unthought of... will disclose at last the secrets of their mysterious workings. Plato was right to *readmit every element of speculation which Socrates had discarded. The problems of universal being are not unattainable, or worthless if attained. But the latter can be solved only by mastering those elements that are now looming on the horizons of the profane. Even the Spiritualists, with their mistaken, grotesquely perverted views and notions, are hazily realising the new situation. They prophecy—and their prophecies are not always without a point of truth in them—or intuitional prevision, so to say.* Hear some of them reasserting the old, old axiom that 'ideas rule the world,' and as men's minds receive new ideas, laying aside the old and effete, the world *will* advance, mighty revolutions *will* spring from them; *institutions, aye, and even* creeds and powers, *they may add*, will crumble before their onward march, crushed by their *own inherent force*, not the irresistible force of the 'new ideas' *offered by the Spiritualists. Yes, they are both right and wrong. It will be 'just as impossible to resist their influence when the time comes as to stay the progress of the tide—to be sure. But what the Spiritualists fail to perceive, I see, and their spirits to explain (the latter knowing no more than what they can find in the brain of the former) is that all this* will come gradually on, and *that* before it comes they, *as well us ourselves*, have all a duty *to perform*, a *task* set before us—that of sweeping away as much as possible the dross left to us by our pious forefathers. New ideas have to be planted on clean places, for these ideas touch upon the most momentous subjects. It is not physical phenomena, *or the agency called Spiritualism*, but these universal ideas that *we have precisely to study; the noumenon, not the phenomenon*: for to comprehend the *latter* we have first to understand the *former*. They *do* touch man's true position in the universe, to be sure, *but only in* relation to his *future* not *previous* births. It is not *physical phenomena, however wonderful, that can ever explain to man* his origin, *let alone* his ultimate destiny, *or as one of them expresses it*, the relation of the mortal to the immortal, of the temporary to the eternal, of the finite to the infinite, etc. *They talk very glibly of what they regard as new ideas*, 'larger, more general, grander, more comprehensive,' *and at the same time they recognise instead* of the eternal reign of immutable law, *the universal reign of law and the expression of a Divine will. Forgetful of their "earlier beliefs, and that 'it repented the Lord that he had made man,' these would-be philosophers and reformers would impress upon their hearers that the expression of the said Divine will 'is unchanging and unchangeable,* in regard to which there is only an Eternal Now, while to mortals[2] time is past or future as related to their finite existence on this material *plane,'—of which they know as little as of their spiritual spheres—a speck of dirt they have made the latter, like our own earth, a future life that the true philosopher would rather avoid than court. But I dream with my eyes open... At all events, this is not any privileged teaching of their own. Most of these ideas are taken piecemeal from Plato and the Alexandrian philosophers*. It is what we all study, and what many have solved, etc., etc.

"This is the true copy of the original document as now restored the 'Rosetta stone' of the Kiddle incident. And now, if you have understood my explanations about the process, as given in a few words further back, you need not ask me how it came to pass that, though somewhat disconnected, the sentences transcribed by the *chela* are mostly those that are now considered as plagiarised, while the missing links are precisely those phrases that would have shown the passages were simply reminiscences, if not quotations—the keynote around which came grouping my own reflections on that morning. For the first time in my life I had paid a serious attention to the utterances of the poetical 'media' of the so-called, 'inspirational' oratory of the English-American lecturers, its quality and limitations. I was struck with all this brilliant but empty verbiage, and recognised for the first time fully its pernicious intellectual tendency. It was their gross and unsavoury materialism, hiding clumsily under its shadowy spiritual veil, that attracted my thoughts at the time. While dictating the sentences quoted—a small portion of the many I have been pondering over for some days—it was those ideas that were thrown out *en relief* the most, leaving out my own parenthetical remarks to disappear in the precipitation."

I need only add a few words of apology to Mr. Kiddle for my accidental neglect of his original communication on this subject addressed to me in India. When his letter above quoted appeared in *Light*, I had no recollection, whatever of having received any letter from him while in India; but within the last few months going over, in London, and sorting papers brought back *en masse* from India, I have turned up the forgotten note. While in India, and the editor of a daily newspaper, my correspondence was such that letters requiring no immediate action on my part would inevitably sometimes be put aside after a hasty glance, and would unfortunately sometimes escape attention afterwards. And after the appearance of this book, I received letters of inquiry of various kinds from all parts of the world, which I was too often prevented by other calls on my time from answering as I should have wished. With the tone and spirit in which Mr. Kiddle made his very natural inquiry I have no fault to find whatever, and if his subsequent letter to *Light* betrayed some disposition on his part to construct unfavourable hypotheses on the basis of the parallel passages, even this second letter would hardly in itself have justified some of the indignant protests ultimately published on the other side. The spiritualists *pur sang*, eager to seize on an incident which seemed to cast discredit on the Theosophical teachings by which their views had been so seriously compromised, were responsible for handling the 'Kiddle incident', in such a way as to provoke the vehement rejoinders of some Theosophical correspondents writing in the columns of *Light* and elsewhere. In consideration, however, of the explanations to which it has eventually given rise, and of the further insight thus afforded us into some interesting details connected with the methods under which an adept's correspondence may sometimes be conducted, the whole incident need not altogether be regretted.

The relations with the "Occult World" that I have been fortunate enough to establish have so greatly expanded during the few years that have elapsed since this volume was written that I must refer my readers to my second book, "Esoteric Buddhism," for an account of their later development. It may be worth while, however, as directly connected with the main purpose of this earlier narrative, to insert here some papers I wrote quite recently for submission to Theosophical audiences in London on the main question discussed in this volume, the existence and sources of knowledge at the command of the adepts. The evidence on this subject has long since overshadowed in its amplitude and completeness the preliminary testimony afforded by my own experiences in India. I summed up some of this later evidence on one of the occasions just referred to, as follows:—

> All persons who become interested in any of the teachings which have found their way out into the world through the intermediation of the Theosophical Society very soon turn to the sanctions on which those teachings rest.
>
> Now the orthodox occult reply hitherto given to inquirers as to the authenticity of any small statements of occult science that have hitherto been put forth, has simply been this: —"Ascertain for yourself." That is to say, lead the pure spiritual life, cultivate the inner faculties, and by degrees these will be awakened and developed to the extent of enabling you to probe Nature for yourself. But that advice is not of a kind which great numbers of people have ever been ready to take, and hence knowledge concerning the truths of occult science has remained in the hands of a few.
>
> A new departure has now been taken. Certain proficients in occult science have broken through the old restrictions of their order, and have suddenly let out a flood of statements into the world, together with some information concerning the attributes and faculties they have themselves acquired, and by means of which they have learned what they now tell us.
>
> It, is very widely recognised that the teaching is interesting and coherent and even supported by analogies, but every new inquirer in turn must ask what assurance we can have that the persons from whom this teaching emanates are in a position to ascertain so much. Most people, I think, would be ready to admit that persons invested, as the Brothers of Theosophy are said to be invested with abnormal and extraordinary powers over Nature—even in the departments of Nature with which we are familiar—may very probably have faculties which enable them to obtain a deep insight into many of the generally hidden truths of Nature. But then come the primary question, "What assurance can you give us that there really are behind the few people who stand forward as the visible representatives of the Theosophical Society, any such persons as the Adept Brothers at all?" This is an old question which is always recurring, and which must go on recurring as long as new comers continue to approach the threshold of the Theosophical Society. For many of us it has long been settled; for some new inquirers the existence of psychological Adepts seems so

probable that the assurances of the leading representatives of the Society in India are readily accepted but for others again, the existence of the Brothers must first be established by altogether plain and unequivocal evidence before it will seem worth while to pay attention to the report some of us make as to the specific doctrine they teach.

I propose, therefore, to go over the evidence on this main question, which certainly underlies any with which the Theosophical Society, so far as it is concerned with the Indian teaching, can be engaged. Of course, I am not going to trouble you with any repetition of particular incidents already described in published writings. What I propose to do is briefly to review the whole case as it now stand, very greatly enlarged and strengthened as it has been during the last two years. The evidence, to begin with, divides itself into two kinds. First, we have the general body of current belief, which in India goes to show that such persons as Mahatmas or Adepts are *somewhere* in existence; secondly, the specific evidence which shows that the leaders of the Theosophical Society are in relation with, and in the confidence of, such Adepts.

As to the general body of belief, it would hardly be too much to say that the whole mass of the sacred literature of India rests on belief in the existence of Adepts and a very widely spread belief, covering great areas of space and time, can rarely be regarded as evolved from nothing—as having had no basis of fact. But passing over the Mahabharata and the Puranas and all they tell us concerning "Rishis or Adepts of ancient date, I may call your attention to a paper in the *Theosophist* of May 1882, on some relatively modern popular Indian books, recounting the lives of various "Sadhus," another word for saint, yogee, or Adept, who have lived within the last thousand years. In this article a list is given of over seventy such persons, whose memory is enshrined in a number of Marathi book", where the miracles they are said to have wrought are recorded. The historical value of their narratives may, of course, be disputed. I mention them merely as illustrations of the fact that belief in the persons having the power now ascribed to the Brothers is no new thing in India. And next we have the testimony of many modern writers concerning the very remarkable occult feats of Indian yogees and fakirs. Such people, of course, are immeasurably below the psychological rank of those whom we speak of as Brothers, but the faculties they possess, sometimes, will be enough to convince anyone who studies the evidence concerning them that living men can acquire powers and faculties commonly regarded as superhuman.

In Jaccolliot's books about his experiences in Benares and elsewhere, this subject is fully dealt with, and some facts connected with it have even forced their way into Anglo-Indian official records. The Report of an English resident at the court of Runjeet Singh describes how he was present at the burial of a yogee who was shut up in a vault, by his own consent, for a considerable period-six weeks, I think, but I have not got the report at hand just now to quote in detail—and emerged alive, at the end of that time, which he had spent in *Samadhi* or trance. Such a man would, of course be an "Adept" of a very inferior type, but the record of his achievements has the advantage of being very well authenticated as far as it goes. Again, up to within a few years ago, a very highly spiritualized ascetic and gifted seer was living at Agra, where he taught a group of disciples, and by their own statement has frequently reappeared amongst them since his death. This event itself was an effort of will accomplished at an appointed time. I have heard a good deal about him from one of his principal followers, a cultivated and highly respected native Government official, now living at Allahabad. His existence, and the fact that he possessed great psychological gifts, are quite beyond question.

Thus, in India, the fact that there are such people in the world as Adepts is hardly regarded as open to dispute. Most of those, of course, concerning whom one can obtain definite information, turn out on inquiry to be yogees of the inferior type, men who have trained their inner faculties to the extent of possessing various abnormal powers, and even insight into spiritual truths.' But none the less do all inquiries after Adepts superior to them in attainments provoke the reply that certainly there are such, though they live in complete seclusion, The general vague, indefinite belief, in fact, paves the way to the inquiry with which we are more immediately concerned— whether the leaders of the Theosophical Society are really in relation with some of the higher Adepts who do not habitually live amongst the community at large, nor make known the fact of their adeptship to any but their own regularly accepted pupils.

Now the evidence on this point divides itself as follows:

First, We have the primary evidence of witnesses who have personally seen certain of these Adepts, both in the flesh and out of the flesh, who have seen their powers exercised, and who have obtained certain knowledge as to their existence and attributes.

Secondly. The evidence of those who have seen them in the astral form, identifying them in various ways with the living men others have seen.

Thirdly. The testimony of those who have acquired circumstantial evidence as to their existence.

Foremost among the witnesses of the first group stand Madame Blavatsky and Colonel Olcott themselves. For those who see reason to trust Madame Blavatsky, her testimony is, of course ample and precise, and altogether satisfactory. She has lived among the Adepts for many years. She has been in almost daily communication with them ever since. She has returned to them, and they have visited her in their natural bodies on several occasions since she emerged from Tibet after her own initiation. There is an intermediate alternative between the conclusion that her statements concerning the Brothers are broadly true, and the conclusion that she is what some American enemies have called her, "the champion impostor of the age." I am aware of the theory which some Spiritualists entertain to the effect that she may be a medium controlled by spirits whom she mistakes for living men, but this theory can only be held by people who are quite inattentive to nine-tenths of the statements she makes, not to speak yet of the testimony of others. How can she have lived under the roof of certain persons in Tibet for seven years and more, seeing them and their friends and relation" going about the business of their daily lives, instructing her by slow degrees in the vast science to which she is devoted, and be in any doubt as to whether they are living men or spirits. The conjecture is absurd. She is either speaking falsely when she tells us that she has so lived among them, or the Adepts who taught her are living men. The Spiritualists hypothesis about her supposed "controls" is built upon the statement she makes, that the Adepts appear to her in the astral form when she is at a distance from them. If they had never appeared to her in any other form there would be room to argue the matter from the Spiritualists' point of view, or there might be, but for other circumstances again. But her astral visitors are identical in all respects with the men she has lived and studied amongst, At intervals, as I have said, she has been enabled to go back again and see them in the flesh. Her astral communication with them merely fills up the gap of her personal intercourse with them, which has extended over a long series of years. Her veracity may of course be challenged, though I think it can be shown that it is most unreasonable to challenge this, but we might as reasonably doubt the living reality of our nearest relations, of the people we live amongst most intimately, as suppose that Madame Blavatsky can be herself mistaken in describing the Brothers as living men. Either she must be right, or has consciously been weaving an enormous network of falsehood in all her writings, acts, and conversations for the last eight or nine years And the plea that she may be a loose talker and given to exaggeration will no more meet the difficulty than the Spiritualists' hypothesis. Pare away as much as you like from the details of Madame Blavatsky's statement on account of possible exaggeration, and that which remains is a great solid block of residual statement which must be either true, or a structure of conscious falsehood. And even if Madame Blavatsky's testimony stood alone, we should have the wonderful fact of her self-sacrifice in the cause of Theosophy to make the hypothesis of her being a conscious impostor one of the most extravagant that could be entertained. At first, when we in India who specially became her friends pointed this out, people said, "But how do you know that she had anything to sacrifice? she may have been an adventurer from the beginning."We proved this conjecture as I have fully explained in my preface to the second edition of the "Occult World", and from some of the foremost people in Russia, her relations and affectionate friends, came abundant assurances of her personal identity. If she had not given up her life to Occultism she might have spent it in luxury among her own people, and in fact as a member of the aristocratic class.

Difficult as the hypothesis of her imposture thus becomes, we next find it in flagrant incompatibility with all the facts of Colonel Olcott's life. As undeniably as in the case of Madame Blavatsky, he has forsaken a life of worldly prosperity to lead the theosophical life, under circumstances of great physical self-denial, in India. And he also tells us that he has seen the Brothers, both in the flesh and in the astral form. By a long series of the most astounding thaumaturgic displays when he was first introduced to the subject in America, he was made acquainted with their powers. He has been visited at Bombay by the living man, his own special master, with whom he had first become acquainted by seeing him in the astral form in America. His life, for years, has been surrounded with the abnormal occurrences which Spiritualists again will sometimes conjecture—so wildly—to be Spiritualism, but which all hinge on to that continuous chain of relationship with the Brothers, which for Colonel Olcott has been partly a matter of occult phenomena, and partly a matter of waking intercourse between man and man. Again, in reference to Colonel Olcott, as in reference to Madame Blavatsky, I assert, fearlessly, that there is no compromises possible between the extravagant assumption that he is consciously lying in all he says about the Brothers, and the assumption that what he says establishes the existence of the Brothers as a broad fact, for remember that Colonel Olcott has now been a co-worker of Madame Blavatsky's and in constant intimate association with her for eight years. The notion the she has been able to deceive him all this while by fraudulent tricks, apart from its monstrosity in other ways, is too unreasonable to be entertained. Colonel Olcott, at all events, knows whether Madame Blavatsky is fraudulent or genuine, and he has given up his whole life to the service of the cause she represents in testimony of his conviction that she is genuine. Again the spiritualistic hypothesis comes into play. Madame Blavatsky may be a medium whose presence surrounds Colonel Olcott with phenomena; but then she is herself deceived by astral influences as to the true nature of the Brothers who are the head and front of the whole phenomenal display, and we have already seen reason, I think, to reject that hypothesis as absurd. There is logical escape from the conclusion that things are broadly as she and Colonel Olcott say, or they are both conscious impostors, rival champions of the age in this respect, both sacrificing everything that worldly minded people live for, to revel in this lifelong imposture which brings them nothing but hard living and hard words.

But the case for the authenticity of their statement, far from ending here, may in one sense be said to begin here. Our native Indian witnesses now come to the front. First, Damodar of whom the well known writer of "Hints on Esoteric Theosophy speaks as follows in that pamphlet:—

"You specially in a former letter referred to Damodar, and you asked how it could be believed that the Brothers would waste time with a half-educated slip of a boy like him, and yet absolutely refuse to visit and convince men like------ and ------, Europeans of the highest education and marked abilities. But do you know that this slip of a boy has deliberately given up high caste, family and friends, and an ample fortune, all in pursuit of the truth. That be has for years lived that pure, unworldly self-denying life which we are told is essential to direct intercourse with the Brothers? 'Oh, a monomaniac,' you say; 'of course he sees anything and everything. But do not you see whither this leads you? Men who do not lead the life do not obtain direct proof of the existence of the Brothers. A man does lead the life and avers that he has obtained such proof, and you straightaway call him a monomaniac, and refuse his testimony,.... quite a "heads I win, tails you lose, 'sort of position."

Damodar has seen some of the Brothers visit the headquarters of the Society in the flesh. He has repeatedly been visited by them in the astral shape. He has himself gone through certain initiations; he has acquired very considerable powers, for he has been rapidly developed as regards these, expressly that he might be an additional link of connection, independently of Madame Blavatsky, between the Brothers, his masters, and the Theosophical Society. The whole life be leads is impressive testimony to the fact that he also *knows* the reality of the Brothers. On another hypothesis we must include Damodar in the conscious imposture supposed to be carried on by Madame Blavatsky, for he has been her intimate associate and devoted assistant, sharing her meals, doing her work, living under her roof at Bombay for several years.

Shall we, then, rather than believe in the Brothers accept the hypothesis that Madame Blavatsky, Colonel Olcott, and Damodar are a band of conscious impostors? In that case Ramaswamy has to he accounted for. Ramaswamy is a very respectable, educated, English-speaking native of Southern India, in government service as a registrar of a court in Tinnevelly, I believe. I have met him several times. First, to indicate the course of his experience in a few words, — he sees the astral form of Madame Blavatsky's Guru, at Bombay; then he gets clairaudient communication with him, while many hundred miles away from all the Theosophists, at his own home in the South of India. Then he travels in obedience to that voice to Darjeeling; then be plunges wildly into the Sikkim jungles in search of the Guru, whom he has reason to believe in that neighbourhood, and after various adventures meets him, —the same man be has seen before in astral shape, the same man whose portrait Colonel Olcott has, and whom be has seen, the living speaker of the voice that has been leading him on from Southern India—He has a long interview with him, a waking, open-air, daylight interview, with a living man, and returns his devoted *chela*, as he is at this moment, and assuredly ever will be. Yet his master, who called him from Tinnevelly and received him in Sikkim, is of those who on the spiritualistic hypothesis are Madame Blavatsky's spirit controls.

Two more witnesses who personally know the Brothers next come to me at Simla, in the persons of two regular *chelas* who have been sent across the mountains on some business, and are ordered *en passant* to visit me and tell me about their master, my Adept correspondent. These men had just come, when I first saw them, from living with the Adepts. One of them, Dhabagiri Nath, visited me several days running, talked to me for hours about Koot Hoomi—with whom he had been living for ten years, and impressed me and one or two others who saw him as a very earnest, devoted, and trustworthy person. Later on, during his visit to India, he was associated with many striking occult phenomena directed to the satisfaction of native inquirers. He, of course, must be a false witness, invented to prop up Madame Blavatsky's vast imposture, if he is anything else than the *chela* of Koot Hoomi that he declares himself to be.

Another native, Mohini, soon after this, begins to get direct communication from Koot Hoomi independently altogether of Madame Blavatsky, and when hundreds of miles away from her. He also becomes a devoted adherent to the Theosophical cause; but Mohini must, as far as I am aware, be ranked in the second group of our witnesses, those who have had personal astral communication with the Brothers, but have not yet seen them in the flesh.

Bhavani Rao, a young native candidate for *chelaship*, who came once in company with Colonel Olcott, but at a time when Madame Blavatsky was in another part of India, to see me at Allahabad, and spent two nights under our roof there, is another witness who has had independent communication with Koot Hoomi, and more than that, who is able himself to act as a link of communication between Koot Hoomi and the outer world, For during the visit I speak of, he was enabled to pass a letter of mine to the master, to receive back his reply, to get off a second note of mine, and to receive back a little note of a few words in reply again. I do not mean that he did all this of his own power, but that his magnetism was such as to enable Koot Hoomi to do it through him. The experience is valuable because it affords a striking illustration of the fact that Madame Blavatsky is not an essential intermediary in the correspondence between myself and my revered friend. Other illustrations are afforded by the frequent passage of letters between Koot Hoomi and myself through the mediation of Damodar at Bombay, at a time when both Madame Blavatsky and Colonel Olcott were away at Madras, travelling about on a Theosophical tour, in the course of which their presence at various places was constantly mentioned in the local papers, I was at Allahabad, and I used, during that time, to send my letters for Koot Hoomi to Damodar at Bombay, and occasionally receive replies so promptly that it would have been impossible for these to have been furnished by Madame Blavatsky, then four or more days further from me in the course of post than Bombay.

In this way, my very voluminous correspondence is, demonstrably as regards portions of it, and therefore by irresistible inference as regards the whole, *not* the work of Madame Blavatsky, or Colonel Olcott, which, if the Brothers are not a reality, it must be, The correspondence is visible on paper, a considerable mass of it, How has it come into existence; reaching me at different places and times, and in different countries, and through different people? I do not quite understand what hypotheses can be framed by a nonbeliever in the Brothers about my correspondence. I can think of none which are not at once negatived by some of the facts about It.

It would be useless to copy out from statements that from time to time have been published in the *Theosophist* the names of native witnesses who have seen the astral forms of the Brothers—spectral shapes which they were informed were such—about the headquarters of the Society at Bombay. Quite a cloud of witnesses would testify to such experiences, and I myself, I may add, saw such an appearance on one occasion at the Society's present headquarters in Madras. But, of course, it might be suggested of such appearances that they were spiritualistic. On the other hand, in that case the argument travels back to the considerations already pointed out, which show that the occult phenomena surrounding Madame Blavatsky cannot be Spiritualism. They can be, in fact, nothing but what we who know her intimately and are now closely identified with the Society believe them to be with all conviction—viz., manifestations of the abnormal psychological powers of those whom we speak of as the Brothers.

As I write, Colonel Olcott and Mr. Mohini Mohun Chatterjee, mentioned above, are in London on a short visit, and many people have heard from their own lips the verification of what I have here stated—as far as it concerns them—and a great deal more besides. For during his recent tour in Northern India, Colonel Olcott had an opportunity of meeting the Mahatma Koot Hoomi personally in the flesh, and thus identifying his previous "astral" visitor. At the same time that this meeting took place, Mr. W. T. Brown, a young Scotchman who has recently become a devoted adherent to the Theosophical cause, also saw the Mahatma, and Mr. Lane Fox, who has gone out to India to follow up the clue afforded by the Theosophical Society, has been in receipt in India, by abnormal methods, of correspondence from Koot Hoomi, while Madame Blavatsky and Colonel Olcott have been in Europe. Taking into account, in fact, over and above the evidence collected in these pages, the abundant information connected with the adepts which has latterly been poured out through the pages of the

Theosophist, the magazine of the Theosophical Society now published at Madras, the argument in the form in which it is here presented is really out of date. Anyone who may still think with Mr. Kiddle, if he remains of the opinion expressed in his letter to *Light*, that the allegations of my book concerning the existence of the adepts and the facts of adeptship still remain to be proved, must be inaccessible to the force of reason, or still unacquainted with the literature of the subject.

The second of the papers I wish to insert here, read like the first to a meeting of the Theosophists in London, dealt with the considerations which, after the *existence* of the Brothers is established, lead us to put confidence in the teaching they convey to us in regard to the origin and destinies of man and the whole problem of Nature. It is as follows:—

> Many people who approach the consideration of occult philosophy are inclined to lay great emphasis on the difference between believing in the existence of those whom we call "the Brothers," and believing in the vast and complicated body of teaching which has now been accumulated by their recent pupils. I think it can really be shown that there is no halting place at which a man who sets out on this enquiry can rationally pause and say, '"Thus far will I go, and no farther". The chain of considerations which will lead anyone who has once realised the existence of the Adepts to feel sure that there can be no great error in a conception of nature obtained with their help, consists of many links, but is really unbroken in its continuity, and equally capable of bearing a strain at any point.
>
> It consists of many links, partly because no one at present among those who are in our position as students—who are living, that is to say, an ordinary worldly life all the while that they are intellectually studying Occultism—can ever obtain in his own person a complete knowledge of the Adepts. He cannot, that is to say, come to know of his own personal knowledge all about even any one Adept. The full elucidation of this difficulty leads to a proper comprehension of the principle on which the Adepts shroud themselves in a partial seclusion, a seclusion which has only become partial within a very recent period, and was so complete until then that the world at large was hardly aware of the existence of any esoteric knowledge from which it could be shut out. This is a matter that is all the more important because experience has shown how the world at large has been quick to take offence at the hesitating and imperfect manner in which the Adepts have hitherto dealt with those who have sought spiritual instruction at their hands. Judging the occult policy pursued

by comparison with inquiries on the plane of physical knowledge, the impatience of inquirers is very natural, but nonetheless does even a limited acquaintance with the conditions of mystic research show the occult policy to be reasonable likewise.

Of course, everyone will admit that Adepts are justified in exercising great caution in regard to communicating any peculiar scientific knowledge which would put what are commonly called magical powers within the reach of persons not morally qualified for their exercise. But the considerations that prescribe this caution do not seem to operate also in reference to the communication of knowledge concerning the spiritual progress of man or the grander processes of evolution. And in truth the Adepts have come to that very conclusion; they have undertaken the communication to the general public of their safe theoretical knowledge, and the effort they are making merely hangs fire, or may seem to do so to some observers, by reason of the magnitude of the task in hand, and the novel aspect it wears, as well for the teachers as for the students. For remember, if there has been that change of policy on the part of the Adepts to which I have just referred, it has been a change of such recent origin that it may almost be described as only just coming on. And if the question be then asked, Why has this safe theoretical knowledge not been communicated sooner, it seems reasonable to find a reply to that question in the actual state of the intellectual world around us at this moment. The freedom of thought of which English writers often boast is not very widely diffused over the world as yet; and hardly, at all events, in any generation before this, could the free promulgation of quite revolutionary tenets in religious matters have been safely undertaken in any country. Communities in which such an undertaking would still be fraught with peril are even now more numerous than those in which it could be set on foot with any practical advantage. One can thus readily understand how in the occult world the question has been one of debate up to our own time, whether it was desirable as yet to promote the dissemination of esoteric philosophy in the world at large at the risk of provoking the acrimonious controversies, and even more serious disturbances, liable to arise from the premature disclosure of truths which only a small minority would really be ready to accept. Keeping this in view, the mystery of the Adepts reserve, up till recently, can hardly be thought so astounding as to drive us on violent alternative hypotheses at variance with all the plain evidence concerning their present action. There is manifest reason why they should be careful in launching a body of newly-won disciples on to their general stream of human progress; and added to this, the force of their own training is such as to make them habitually cautious to a far greater extent than the utmost prudence of ordinary life would render ordinary men. "But," it will be argued, "granting all this, but assuming, that at last some of the Adepts, at all events, have come to the conclusion that some of their knowledge is ripe for presentation to the world, why do they not present as much as they do present, under guarantees of a more striking, irresistible, and conclusive kind than those which have actually been furnished?" I think the answer may be easily drawn from the consideration of the way in which it would be natural to expect that a change of policy amongst the Adepts in a matter of this kind would gradually be introduced. By the hypothesis we conceive them but just coming to the conclusion that it is desirable to teach mankind at large some portions of that spiritual science hitherto conveyed exclusively to those who give tremendous pledges in justification of their claim to acquire it. They will naturally advance, in dealing with the world at large, along the same lines they have learned to trust in dealing with aspirants for regular initiation. Never in the history of the world have they sought out such aspirants, courted them or advertised for them in any way whatever. It has been found an invariable law of human progress that some small percentage of mankind will always come into the world invested by Nature with some of the attributes proper to adeptship, and with minds so constituted as to catch conviction as to the possibilities of the occult life, from the least little sparks of evidence on the subject that may be floating about. Of persons so constituted some have always been found to press forward into the ranks of *chelaship*, to resort, that is to say, to any devices or opportunities that circumstances may afford them for fathoming occult knowledge. When thus besieged by the aspirant the Adept has always, sooner or later, disclosed himself. The change of policy now introduced prescribes that the Adept shall make one step towards the disclosure of himself in advance of the aspirant's demand upon him, but we can easily understand how the Adept, in first making this change, would argue that if many *chelas* have hitherto come forward in the absence of any spontaneous action from his side, it might be that an almost dangerous rush of ill qualified aspirants would be invited by any manifestation from him that should be more than a very slight one. At any rate, the Adept would say it would be premature to begin by too sensational a display of faculties inherent in advanced spiritual knowledge with which the world at large is as yet unfamiliar. It will be better at first to make such an offer as will only be calculated to inflame the imagination of persons only one step removed beyond those whose natural instincts would lead them into the occult life. This appears actually to have been the reasoning on which the Adepts have proceeded so far, and this may help us to understand how it is that, as I began by saying, no one person amongst those outer students, who have been called lay-*chelas*, has yet been enabled to say that of his own personal knowledge he knows all about any of the Adepts.

On the other hand, putting together the various scattered revelations concerning the Brothers which have been distributed amongst various people in India belonging to the Theosophical Society, so much can be learned about the Adepts as to put us in a very strong position in regard to estimating their qualifications for speaking with confidence as they do about the actual facts of Nature on the superphysical plane. These scattered revelations—if my reasoning in what has gone before may be accepted—have been broken up and thrown about in fragments designedly, in order that as yet it should only be possible to arrive at a full conviction concerning Adeptship after a certain amount of trouble spent in piecing together the disjointed proofs. But when this process is accomplished we are provided with a certain block of knowledge concerning the Adepts, out of which large inferences must necessarily grow. We find, to begin with, that they do unequivocally possess the power of cognizing event and facts on the physical plane of knowledge with which we are familiar, by other means than those connected with the five senses. We find also that they unequivocally possess the power of emerging from their proper bodies and appearing at distant places in more or less ethereal counterparts thereof which are not only agencies for producing impressions on others but habitations for the time being of the Adepts' own thinking principles, and thus in themselves, if the proof went no further, demonstration of the fact that a human soul is something quite independent of brain matter and nerve centres. I do not stop now to enumerate instances. The record of evidence must be dissociated from its manipulation in arguments like the present, but the records are abundant and accessible for all who will take the trouble of examining them. Now, if we know that the Adept's soul can pass at his own discretion into that state in which its perceptive faculties are independent of corporeal machinery, it is not surprising that he should be enabled to make, of his own knowledge, a great many statements concerning processes of Nature, reaching far beyond any knowledge that can be obtained by mere physical observation. Take for example, the Adepts' statement that certain other planets besides this earth, are concerned with the growth of the great crop of humanity of which we form a part. This is not advanced as a conjecture or inference. The Adepts tell us that once out of the body they find they can cognize events on some other planets as well as in distant parts of our own. This is not the exceptional belief of an exceptionally organised individual, who may be regarded by doubters as hallucinated; there is no room for doubting the fact that it is the concurrent testimony' of a considerable body of men engaged in the constant experimental exercise of similar faculties. In this way the fact becomes as much a fact of true science, as the fact that the great nebula Orion, for instance, exhibits a gaseous spectrum, and is therefore a true nebula. All of us who have star spectroscope can ascertain that fact for ourselves, if we make use of a clear night when the conditions of observation are possible. To doubt it, would not be to show greater caution than is exercised by those who believe it, but merely an imperfect appreciation of the evidence. It is true that in regard to the condition of the other planets our acceptance of the Adepts' statement must be governed by our impressions concerning the *bona fides* of their intention in telling us that they have made such and such observations. So far it is a matter of inference with us whether the Adepts are saying what *they believe* to be true—when they speak of the septenary chain of planets to which the earth belongs— or consciously deluding us with a rigmarole of statements which they know to be false. I think it can be shown in a variety of ways, that the latter supposition is absurd. But an exhaustive examination of its absurdity would be a considerable task in itself. For the moment the position I am endeavouring to establish is one which does not depend upon the question whether the Adepts are telling us, in reference to the planets, what they know to be true, or something which they know to be untrue. My present position is that at all events the Adepts themselves know what is true In the matter, and that position, it will be observed, is not vitiated by the fact that, as yet, we, their most recent pupils, are unable to follow In their footsteps and repeat the experiments on which their teaching rests.

The same train of reasoning may be applied to the whole body of teaching which the Theosophical Society is now concerned in endeavouring to assimilate. As offered now to the uninitiated world, it can only take the form of a set of statement on authority. And that sort of statement is not one which is most agreeable to our methods or to the Adepts' habitual methods of teaching. For there is no chemical laboratory in England where the system of teaching Is more rigidly confined to the direction of the learner's own experiments, than that same system is adopted with occult *chelas* following the regular course of initiation. Step by step, as the regular *chela* is told that such and such is the fact in regard to the inner mysteries of Nature, he is shown how to apply his own developing faculties to the direct observation of such facts, But those developing faculties carry with them, as pointed out a while ago, fresh powers over Nature which can only be entrusted to those from whom the Adepts take the recognised pledges. In teaching outsiders as they are trying to do now, the Adepts *must* depart from their own habitual methods, —we must depart, if we wish to understand what they are willing to teach, from our habitual methods of inquiry. We must suspend our usual demand for proof of each statement made, in turn as it is advanced. We must rest our provisional trust in each statement on our broad general conviction which can be satisfied along familiar lines of demonstration, —that such men as the Adepts certainly exist, even though we cannot visit them at pleasure, that they must understand an enormous block of Nature's laws outside the range of those which the physical senses cognize, that in any statement they make to us they must be in a position to know absolutely whether that statement is or is not true.

This much fully realised, the truth is that each inquirer in turn becomes satisfied, *pari passu* with his realisation of the case so far, that reason revolts against the notion that the Adepts can be engaged in their present attempt to convey some of their own knowledge to the world at large in any other than the purest good faith. It may be concluded that we who have come to the conclusion that their teaching is altogether to be accepted, are rearing a large inverted pyramid upon a small base. But the logical strength of our position is not impaired by this objection. In every branch of human knowledge, inferences far transcend the observed facts out of which they grow. And even in the most exact science of all, a theorem is held to be proved if any alternative hypothesis is found, on examination to be irrational. Moreover, the doctrine even of legal testimony recognises the value of secondary evidence where in the nature of the case It is impossible that primary evidence can be forthcoming. That is exactly the state of the case in regard to the present attempt to bridge the gulf that separates the school of physical research from the from the school of spiritual knowledge. As long as we of this side were justified in doubting whether there was anywhere on earth such a thing as a school of spiritual knowledge, it may have been hardly worth while to worry ourselves with the stray fragments of its teaching which now and then broke loose in barely intelligible shapes. But to doubt the existence of such a school now is equivalent, really to doubting the statement about the nebula in Orion, according to the illustration I adduced just now. It can only arise from inattention to the facts of the whole case as these now stand, —from reluctance to take that *trouble* to examine these thoroughly, which still, as a sort of hedge, separates the Theosophical Society from the general community in the midst of which it is planted. Regarded in the light of an occult barrier, —as an obstacle which corresponds, in the case of the lay—*chela* to the really serious ordeals which have to be crossed by the regular *chela*, —the necessity of taking this trouble can hardly be regarded as a hedge that it is difficult to traverse. And on the other side there lies a wealth of information concerning the mysteries of Nature which clearly lights up vast regions of the past and future hitherto shrouded in total darkness for critical intelligences, and the prey for others of untrustworthy conjecture. For those who once thoroughly go into the matter, and obtain a complete mastery over all the considerations I have put forward, —who thus obtain full conviction the Brothers certainly exist, that they must be acquainted with the actual facts about Nature behind and beyond this life, that they are now ready to convey a considerable block of their knowledge to us, and that it is ridiculous to distrust their *bona fides* in doing this, —for all such true Theosophists of the Theosophical Society, nothing, at present, connected with spiritual success is comparable in importance with the study of the vast doctrine now in process of delivery Into our hands.

---

1. In the original book, but one after the other in this edition.
2. uninitiated

Copyright © 2020 by ALICIA EDITIONS.
No part of this book may be reproduced in any form or by any electronic or mechanical means, including information storage and retrieval systems, without written permission from the author, except for the use of brief quotations in a book review.

www.ingramcontent.com/pod-product-compliance
Lightning Source LLC
LaVergne TN
LVHW040059080526
838202LV00045B/3707